The Modern Anglo-Dutch Empire:

its Origins, Evolution, and Anti-Human Outlook

by Robert Ingraham

"In nations which have made a false commencement, it would be found that the citizen, or rather the subject, has extorted immunity after immunity, as his growing intelligence and importance have both instructed and required him to defend those particular rights which were necessary to his well-being. A certain accumulation of these immunities constitutes... the essence of European Liberty, even at this hour. It is scarcely necessary to tell the reader that this freedom, be it more or less, depends on a principle entirely different from our own. Here the immunities do not proceed from, but they are granted to the government, being, in other words, concessions of natural rights made by the people to the state, for the benefit of social protection. So long as this vital difference exists between ourselves and other nations, it will be vain to think of finding analogies in their institutions. The mildest and justest governments in Europe are, at this moment, theoretically despotisms."

James Fenimore Cooper - *The Bravo*

Table of Contents:

On the Cover – The Little Tower of Babel, Pieter Bruegel the Elder, Museum Boijmans Van Beuningen ©

This work is dedicated to Andrea,
my wife of 38 years

Introduction to 2018 edition

In the fourteen years since this work was written, much has changed in the world, some very bad, but, at the same time, a powerful positive force for the good has been introduced into human affairs. We have collectively witnessed the horrible effects and degeneracy of the George W. Bush and Barack Obama presidencies, which, among other things, have produced ongoing global colonial war, as well as the destruction of the productive capabilities of the trans-Atlantic world, rising death rates, plunging birth rates, and the creation of the greatest speculative financial bubble in history.

However! We are also witnessing a global revolt against imperial financial policies, now spreading and strengthening. Beginning with the 2016 Brexit vote in Britain, followed by the election of Donald Trump in November of that same year, a resistance to "globalization" and a momentum toward a return to national economic sovereignty has emerged as a potential new direction for world affairs.

The problem today is that in both western Europe, as well as the United States, the imperial paradigm still remains hegemonic. There are hopeful signs, but the fight is not yet won. This is an oligarchical paradigm which dominates all of popular culture of the trans-Atlantic region, but also, more dangerously, still controls financial and economic policy from the entrenched power centers of the City of London and Wall Street. We are in both a hopeful but dangerous moment. A battle is now underway as to the future of the United States. Will we jettison the failed imperial policies and axioms of recent decades and join in the project for a productive and prosperous future, or reject it and suffer the consequences?

* * * * *

This edition of *The Modern Anglo-Dutch Empire* is largely identical to what was written more than a decade ago. Minor editing and re-writing occurs in many passages, but the content is coherent with the original. The only two substantive changes to the work are, first, a fuller discussion of Alexander Hamilton's concept of Public Credit, and, second, an effort to more precisely clarify the connection between the monetary and related policies of Empire and the philosophical outlook from which those policies derive.

Robert Ingraham
May, 2018

Preface

This is a book about Empire. In one sense, its primary focus is on the modern manifestation of Empire, i.e., the misunderstood Anglo-Dutch System, which was born in the late 16th century, and came into maturity between 1688-1763. That empire is still very much with us today. In another sense, this book deals with the basic question of the nature of Empire itself, not any particular empire, but the ongoing oligarchical idea of Empire—the oligarchical outlook and culture, so to speak.

Most people today think of empires as something of the past. Were that only true, the world presently would be in a much happier condition. Whether you realize it or not, the issue of Empire, and the human race's long struggle to free itself from the oligarchical structures and culture of Empire is the most critical political concern facing us today. We are currently confronted with a profound economic and strategic crisis, and defeating the current schemes of the Empire is now a matter of life or death for humanity.

Much of this book is very detailed, with names and places that may not be familiar to many. I urge you to be patient, and to work your way through the material. The sections on Rome, Salamanca, John Locke, Empiricism, and banking may seem tedious, but hopefully, when you are finished, you will understand that Empire – and its oligarchical view of mankind – is the mortal enemy of humanity, and that the historical mission of the United States is to eliminate that enemy once and for all.

*   *   *   *   *

Virtually all modern academically-approved histories are incompetent. That statement will probably provoke some PhD recipients to dismiss the following work out of hand, but there are two legitimate reasons for making such a claim. The first reason is the pervasive failure of accredited American, as well as European, historians to appreciate the profound importance of the American Revolution, and the axiomatic species-difference between the American constitutional republic and the British Empire, a difference which persists down to the present day. This mis-perception of the American mission has led to a great deal of confusion, e.g., among Asian and other scholars who mis-identify the oligarchical philosophical outlook of Empire with what is sometimes called "Western Culture." The evidence of this failure is perhaps most glaring in the almost universal inability, or unwillingness, to distinguish between the American methods of national banking and the constitutional issuance of currency, i.e., a Hamiltonian Credit System, contrary to the European system of private central banking and financial gambling.

The second failure of modern historians is the almost universal contamination of historical analysis with a mechanistic-fatalist approach. This latter flaw is particularly glaring with Marxist, as well as various neo/pseudo-Marxist types, but the same condemnation can be made of the Chicago and Vienna schools' incompetent view of impersonal "market forces." Philosophically, the followers of both Marx and Hayek, as well as their many and varied derivatives, are identical in their empirical-mechanistic methodology, and they both share the same "mother,"—19th century British Liberalism.

There is also a deeper issue. The subject of history is Man, but the university libraries are satiated with history books, which evade the most basic obvious question: What is man's nature which sets him apart from the lower beasts, allows him to create both science and great symphonies, and to increase his mastery over the planet? Or to put it more plainly, what is it about man that allows him to even hypothesize about human history, since monkeys, donkeys and whales have no such capability? How can anyone write a competent history of *mankind,* without even addressing that question? How does one understand Man's history, and the long periods of progress, and retrogression which have characterized it, unless one starts with the fundamental question: What does it mean to be human? The literary journals are full of articles, written by university professors who write like bad-imitation Joe Fridays: "Just the Facts." But in reality, such factuality produces lies, because of what it leaves out. This problem has become much worse with the advent of the so-called "information society," a false reality in which real history is butchered by the "fact-checkers" of Wikipedia, and their ilk.

In truth, as hopefully this work will elucidate, the question as to the true nature of the human identity strikes at the very essence of the nature of Empire, and no competent history can be written which does not start from that standpoint.

This book does not pretend to be a "history of the human race from beginning to end," nor does it make any claims of profundity in the realms of science or philosophy, but, if we return to the question, "What is it in Man's nature which sets him apart from the lower beasts?," as we work our way through the history and nature of the Anglo-Dutch Empire, hopefully some glimmers of understanding will come forth.

The subject of this work is the millennia-long struggle of the human race to free itself from Empire: to free itself politically, economically, culturally, and morally. Not from any particular empire, such as the Ottomans or the Persians, but from the continuing ontological reality of an ongoing oligarchical idea of Empire, the which, continues to infest this world in this our 21st century. The specific focus at hand is the modern Anglo-Dutch System of empire, because that is the one which currently threatens mankind's future. The majority of this writing will concentrate on how this monstrosity came into existence and consolidated its power. Hence, the years from 1582 to 1763 will require most of our attention. However, the rise of Venetian power after 1100, as well as the 19th and 20th centuries' British targeting of the American Republic, will also be examined, but not with the same depth of historical detail. The specific structures of the Anglo-Dutch System have evolved over time, but the axiomatic nature of the modern oligarchical empire was complete by 1763. My purpose here is to report on the origins of that Anglo-Dutch System, and to provide insight into its evil nature.

Human voluntarism

All of recorded human history encompasses a centuries-long fight between those who view man as a noble creature, as *Genesis* says: "made in the Creator's image," versus the oligarchic view of man as a beast, expendable, a "worthless wretch."   All human progress has emanated from champions of the first view; empires result from proponents of the second view. To be clear, this is not a connect-the-dots conspiracy theory of history; this is a question of axiomatic views as to the fundamental nature of what it means to be human.

This book defies all mechanistic versions of history. This is very much a voluntaristic view of history, which is, after all, the only human way to view mankind's development. History is not determined by "events," nor by inevitable economic processes. From the pre-historic years when mariners and astronomers first studied the progression of the constellations, mankind's history on – and increasing domination over – the planet, has been shaped by voluntaristic human action, action catalyzed by the creativity of individual human minds. When societies have been imbued with this notion of what it means to be human, civilization has progressed. When empires have dominated, when the few rule the many like cattle, mankind has suffered.

Contrast the following two quotations:

"At present the population of the world is increasing ... War so far has had no great effect on this increase ... I do not pretend that birth control is the only way in which population can be kept from increasing. There are others ... If a Black Death could be spread throughout the world once in every generation, survivors could procreate freely without making the world too full ... the state of affairs might be somewhat unpleasant, but what of it? Really high-minded people are indifferent to suffering, especially that of others."

Bertrand Russell, *The Impact of Science on Society* (1952)

"Reason is that wherein man goes before all other earthly creatures and comes after God only.... For whereas God and nature hath furnished other creatures, some with hoofs, others with other instruments, and weapons both defensive and offensive, man is left naked, and destitute of all these, but may comfort himself in that one endowment of reason, and providence, whereby he is able to govern them all."

John Robinson, Pastor of the Plymouth (Pilgrim) Church, *Of Faith, Hope, and Love, Reason and Sense*

Russell, of course, is not merely a private individual, voicing his own "personal opinions." He is the ultimate personification of the British Empire. His ancestor Edward Russell was a leader in the 1688 Glorious Revolution which brought the Venetian System to London, and his grandfather Lord John Russell was the Victorian British Prime Minister during the years of Britain's genocide against the Irish, known today as the "potato famine," and he also presided over the massive expansion of British opium trafficking into China. As his grandson stated, "high minded people are indifferent to suffering." Lyndon LaRouche has called the British Empire's Bertrand Russell – the same Russell who publicly advocated pre-emptive nuclear war against the Soviet Union[1] – "the most evil man of the 20th century.

John Robinson, together with others such as John Winthrop, Cotton Mather, and Benjamin Franklin, defined a different mission for the American colonists, one grounded in a conception of the human species stridently hostile to Bertrand Russell's mad ravings. As enshrined in the later Declaration of Independence, all human beings are born with the potential for human discovery and creative reason. They operate from an axiomatic view of the nobleness of the human identity. It is precisely this commitment to true

---

[1] In the *Bulletin of Atomic Scientists,* 1948

human happiness which defines the unbridgeable gulf between Empire and Republic.

The following two quotations from Henry C. Carey, the foremost American economist of the mid-to-late 19th century, demonstrate this difference in an historically specific way:

"Two systems are before the world.... One looks to pauperism, ignorance, depopulation, and barbarism; the other to increasing wealth, comfort, intelligence, combination of action, and civilization. One looks toward universal war; the other to universal peace. One is the English system; the other we may be proud to call the American system, for it is the only one ever devised, the tendency of which was that of elevating while equalizing the condition of man throughout the world."

The Harmony of Interests, (1851)

"Hence it is that we see the slave trade prevail to so great an extent in all the countries subject to the British system.... The system to which the world is indebted for these results is called "free trade;" but there can be no freedom of trade where there is no freedom of man, for the first of all commodities to be exchanged is labour, and the freedom of man consists only in the exercise of the right to determine for himself in what manner his labour shall be employed, and how he will dispose of its products.... It [the British System] is the most gigantic system of slavery the world has yet seen, and therefore it is that freedom gradually disappears from every country over which England is enabled to obtain control."

This, then, is the battlefield, the two opposing sides, in a fight that has existed for thousands of years, a fight whose outcome is still undetermined as of today.

1582

In 1582, a political revolution in Venice brought to power the *Giovani* party, associated with the Servite monk Paolo Sarpi. The seeds of this revolution were already planted some years before 1582, but it was with the ascension to power of the Giovani, and the continuing career of Sarpi, up until his death in 1623, that the modern Anglo-Dutch System was born. The locus of this new empire was gradually shifted to northern Europe – first to Amsterdam, then to London – and new theories of finance, trade, international law, and government were created, for the purpose of ensuring continued oligarchical rule. Those theories, and the anti-human philosophical method behind them, continue in practice up to this very day.

1582 was not the beginning of "Empire," but it was the beginning of the modern form of empire, the Anglo-Dutch Liberal System. The philosophical, economic, and scientific ideas that have come down to us from that 1582 revolution are virtually all-encompassing. To be sure, they include concepts of private finance, banking, money and trade, which evolved over decades into what became the British System of "free trade." Many historians, however, overemphasize the mere financial aspects of this imperial system. Of greater importance, it was the philosophical empiricism of Sarpi and his epigone that has had a profound influence over virtually every branch of philosophy, science, and mathematics. Some of those influences will be taken up in this current work. For now, however, the important guidepost to keep before us, is Sarpi's denial of basic human nature. Coherent with the Empire idea of "rule of the few over the many" is the necessity to deny the idea of lawful human creativity. The prospect of a self-governing republic, in which the fostering of human reason, scientific and technological progress, and individual creativity is consciously promoted, is anathema to the Empire crowd. Theirs is an Olympian oligarchical view, and from their standpoint, Sarpi's most invaluable contribution to continued oligarchical rule is his understanding that "mental chains" are more effective then armies in enforcing human servitude.

The falsity of modernism

Frequently, today, it is all-too-common to hear an apologist for the Empire – such as Felix Rohatyn – state that the policies of Franklin Roosevelt are *passé*, a "thing of the past." Putting to one side the ulterior motives of someone like Rohatyn in making such a statement, too many gullible people have been mis-educated in the idea that history progresses in irreversible linear "stages," each of which determines a fixed set of policy options. A lunatic clinical example of this type of thinking is Alvin Toffler's "Third Wave" nonsense. A more widespread type of British propaganda is the assertion that we have moved, again irreversibly, from an industrial to a post-industrial economy, and the related assertion that we have moved from a world of national economies to a globalized economy of limited or non-existent national sovereignty. This is all asserted as irreversible historical fact. The howling irony here is that it is the same people making those assertions – the City of London and Wall Street crowd – who have been attempting, since Richard Nixon abolished the Bretton Woods System in 1971, to turn back the clock on history, to reverse the policies of Franklin Roosevelt, to eradicate the Public Credit System of Alexander Hamilton and Abraham Lincoln, and to GO BACK to a system of private financiers ruling the world.

The 1648 Treaty of Westphalia established a system of relations among perfectly sovereign nation-states. The subsequent American revolution and 1788 U.S. Constitution defined the intent of the new nation to be the promotion of the General Welfare and led to the Hamilton-sponsored policy of willfully increasing the productivity of labor. These were all efforts to free humanity from the degradation of Empire. Since 1876, the Empire crowd has been determined to REVERSE these historical breakthroughs, to return to a pre-1776 world controlled by a private financial elite. Today, this reactionary design is always put forward with the most ardent claims that globalization, "universal democracy," and the information age represent something new, and are ushering in a 21st century enlightened era for humanity. Protective tariffs are declared reactionary; Social Security is declared outmoded; unregulated off-shore banking is defended as an example of the "new freedom." With all of the chutzpah of a carnival barker, the Empire has convinced millions of fools that "snow is black," in their claims that the 21st century manifestations of Empire represent progress and human freedom.

This transparent Empire propaganda is actually a rather tired tactic. It's the same line that British spokesmen used in attacking the protective tariffs of Lincoln and McKinley, and it has been used many times since. Consider what Sun-Yat Sen, the founder of modern China and the great admirer of Abraham Lincoln, said about British designs in 1924:

> "A new theory is emerging in England, proposed by intellectuals, which opposes nationalism on the ground that it is narrow and illiberal; that doctrine is cosmopolitanism... I constantly hear young men saying, '(Sun Yat-Sen's) Principles are not adapted to the tendencies of modern times; the latest and best doctrine is cosmopolitanism.' Is it really?... Cosmopolitanism is the same thing as China's theory of world empire two thousand years ago... (Today) the nations which are employing imperialism to conquer others and which are trying to maintain their own favored positions as sovereign lords of the whole world are advocating cosmopolitanism and want the world to join them"
>
> *The Three Principles of the People*, 1924

Simply substitute the word "globalization" for "cosmopolitanism," and you see the same British imperial outlook, resurrected today, clothed in the language of the 21st century.

The crisis and the opportunity

Today, the modern system of empire is facing a profound existential crisis, perhaps the gravest crisis of its several centuries existence. Its own policies have produced a financial system built on hundreds of trillions of dollars of speculative debt, hyperinflation, chaos, a danger of world war, and – most important of all – a growing resistance by the world's peoples to the continuation of oligarchical rule. More and more people are "looking behind the curtain," and beginning to see that the wizard is really a pathetic bankrupt creature. We are now at a moment of historic opportunity for revolutionary economic, monetary, and cultural change.

The danger to humanity today is great, yet this crisis is also an opportunity, and we can rejoice, that the means exist to rid the world forever of the pestilence of Empire.

In earlier times a work such as this would have been unnecessary. Benjamin Franklin, Alexander Hamilton, John Quincy Adams, Abraham Lincoln, William McKinley and earlier generations of Americans all understood precisely that the System of Empire was the mortal enemy of America. They also understood that the Empire had roots which went far back into human history. Tragically, today this knowledge is largely gone. Hopefully, this work will help to rectify that.

Robert Ingraham
August, 2008

I.   The Bestial View of Man: from Rome to Venice

Emperor Justinian

In 1433, Cardinal Nicholas of Cusa, writing in Book II of his *Concordantia Catholica*, states

> Since Natural Law is based on reason, all law by nature is rooted in the reason of man."

and later in Book III of the same work, he says:

> "There is in the people a divine seed by virtue of their common equal birth and the equal natural rights of all men, so that all authority — which comes from God as does man himself — is recognized as divine when it arises from the common consent of all the subjects. . . . This is that divinely ordained marital state of spiritual union based on a lasting harmony by which a commonwealth is guided in the fullness of peace toward eternal bliss."

This Platonic concept of the divine spark of reason inherent in all human beings – that which distinguishes us from the beasts – is the basis for all modern nation-state republics, including, most emphatically, our own United States. Empire has always striven to extinguish this concept of Man from the planet, and to relegate the human species to the servile conditions which existed under the Roman Empire, or the later Roman-created, feudal system.

The idea of Empire begins in pre-historic times, but it is

the legacy of Babylon, and the paradigmatic role of the Babylonian priesthood as the controllers of religion, banking and culture, which set the model for the ancient world, including the Persian Empire, the role of the Greek Temple at Delphi, the Roman Empire, and Rome's continuation at Byzantium.

In 533 A.D., the Byzantine Emperor Justinian issued the *Corpus Juris Civilis*, a compilation of all of the Roman law codes which had been promulgated over the previous several centuries. To this day, Roman Law, and the bestial view of Man it embodies, defines the Empire view. Roman Law codifies rule by an oligarchy, and it defines "property rights," including the property of human slaves, as the basis for all law. Roman Law remained the imperial legal system of the Byzantine Empire, lasting until 1453.

After the collapse of the Roman Empire in the west, the anti-human outlook of that empire continued, and was concretized in the so-called "feudal system," a system that came into existence as a product of the taxation and related codes of the Roman Emperor Diocletian, who ruled from 284 to 305 A.D. It was Diocletian's "reforms" which established the legal and economic basis for the emergence of feudalism, a system where the vast majority of the European population were bound to the land as little more than two-legged farm animals.[2] This was a system of *de facto* perpetual slavery.

With the emergence of Venetian power in the 11th century, we see the return of an explicit Roman Imperial outlook to Western Europe. During this period, the respective geopolitical roles of Venice and the Byzantine Empire were reversed. Venice, previously a satellite/client state of Constantinople, emerged by 1200 as the dominant

---

[2] "Lessons of the 14th Century Dark Age," by Will Wertz, *Fidelio*, Vol. 7, No. 3, 1998

military and economic force in the Mediterranean. In 1096 Venice organized the first Crusade, to be followed by four more over the next 126 years. Out of these crusades the Venetian empire was born. The infamous fourth Crusade, wherein Venice organized the sack and military occupation of Constantinople in 1204, gave Venice the island of Crete and almost all of the Byzantine colonies along the Adriatic Sea. By the middle of the 13th century, Venetian galleys dominated the Mediterranean and were actively trading in Flanders and London. The Venetian Empire was the leading imperial maritime power in all of Europe.

The medieval *Fondi's* two projects

During this "first Venetian era," two inter-related "cultural" projects were set into motion, both aimed at solidifying and perpetuating oligarchical rule. The first project was the translation of all of Aristotle's extant works into Latin. The second was the revival and republishing of the works that made up Roman Civil Law.

The medieval system that emerged from the partnership of the Venetians and the Norman feudal nobility, and that dominated Europe for centuries, was in a sense, a "world without progress." Wars might be fought, kings might live and die, but the fixed nature of the zero-growth feudal system seemed permanent. Aristotelianism and Roman Law were the two epistemological social control mechanisms perfectly suited for this primitive oligarchical schema. Roman Law established the legal basis for treating the vast majority of the population as non-thinking beasts. Aristotelianism, with its emphasis on "sense certainty," not only denied the Platonic notions of hypothesis and creativity,[3] but also postulated a cosmology of a fixed perfected universe, within which no change or progress were possible.

The medieval revival of Roman Law was the joint product of an alliance between Venice and what became known as the Guelph faction of the feudal nobility. This revival began with the founding of the School of Jurisprudence (later University) at Bologna in 1084, by Matilda of Tuscany (1046-1114). The heiress to immense feudal land-ownings in northern Italy, Matilda was married to Duke Welf V of Bavaria, and it was the wars that Matilda and Welf V fought against the German King Henry IV in northern Italy which gave birth to the Venetian-allied Guelph Party. Her role in the personal humiliation of Henry IV earned her the sobriquet of Matilda of Canossa.[4]

Matilda of Tuscany:
Godmother to the Black Guelphs

---

[3] Earlier, through St. Paul, St. Augustine and others, the Platonic nature of Christianity had been explicit.

[4] This Matilda should not to be confused with her near contemporary, the Empress Matilda (1101-1169). This second Matilda was the daughter of the English King Henry I, and the first in line to the English throne. She was married, at the age of 12, to the German Emperor Henry V, but after his death, she re-

Pinpointing the exact date of the Roman Law revival is impossible. Supposedly, an intact copy of Justinian's *Digest* was discovered in the late 11th century, but no one knows exactly when, or who discovered it. What is known for certain is the 1084 deployment, by Matilda, of the Italian jurist Irnerius to found the School of Jurisprudence at Bologna, and that, by the early 12th century, this school had become the European center for all legal studies. The curriculum was based entirely on the study of Roman Law, particularly the *Digest*. Irnerius, himself, lectured on the entire *Corpus Juris Civilis*. His chief work is the *Summa Codicis*, the first systematic application of Roman Law to medieval jurisprudence. Pepo, another early Bologna professor, wrote commentaries on Justinian and other Roman texts. Beginning in the 11th & 12th centuries, various new commentaries, known as "glosses, were also written on the *Corpus Juris Civilis*, and these became extremely influential in their own right.

By the early 13th century there were 10,000 students at Bologna, and the University was known as the *Mater Studiorum*. It was the intellectual center of medieval Europe. Graduates of the University founded many other schools, including Vincenza (1204), Arezzo (1215), and Padua (1222), and at all of these schools, the curriculum mimicked that of Bologna.

Roman Law

Roman Law begins with the concept that all men are

---

married, this time to Geoffrey, the Duke of Anjou. Their progeny became the founders of the Angevin (or Plantagenet) dynasty in England. Matilda's son, King Henry II, ruled over vast feudal holdings in England, Normandy, Aquitaine, Gascony, and Touraine, and Henry's heir, Richard the Lionheart, became the leader of Venice's Third Crusade in 1191. Throughout most of their history the Plantagenets were puppets of Venice's Lombard League.

beasts: "The law of nature is that law which nature teaches to all animals. For this law does not belong exclusively to the human race, but belongs to all animals, whether of the earth, the air, or the water." (*The Institutes; Of Persons*). Under Roman Law, there is no distinction made between humans and beasts. Man is "born into nature" like any other animal, and subject to the same rules. *The Institutes* say that, "By the law of nature all men are originally born free," but this freedom is not the freedom of creatures made in God's image; rather, it is the "freedom" into which wild dogs or savage beasts are born (born free in a state of nature).

Roman Law uses the terms "Natural Law" and "Law of Nature" interchangeably. In Roman usage, Natural Law is not derived from man's capacity to discover the laws of the universe, and to act upon that universe—to continue God's creation, based on the human spark of reason. Rather, "the laws of nature remain ever fixed and immutable." (*The Institutes; Of Persons*). In Roman Law there is a complete absence of physical-economy and man's Promethean role in science. Everything is discussed from the standpoint of man's fixed relation with (and within) nature. In Roman Law, "Natural Law" as Nicholas of Cusa would have expressed it, does not exist.

Since there is no real universal "Natural Law," societies are free to enact laws which infringe upon the "Laws of Nature." For example, "Freedom is the natural power of doing what we each please, unless prevented by force of law... Slavery is an institution of the law of nations, by which one man is made the property of another, contrary to natural right. Slaves are in the power of their masters, a power derived from the law of nations; for among all nations it may be remarked that masters have the power of life and death over their slaves."

This Roman distinction between the Law of Nature and the Law of Nations (man-made law), is the origin of the centuries long debate over Natural Law vs. Positive Law. It should be noted, however, that from Grotius, through Locke, down into the modern era, this debate is axiomatically flawed, because most of those involved are not talking about (Cusa's or Plato's) Natural Law, but the Roman Law of Nature.

The heart and soul of Roman Law is the *Corpus Juris Civilis*, written at the direction of the Emperor Justinian and issued in 533 AD. There were originally three parts to the *Corpus*, with a fourth added later. The first three parts were not written at the time of Justinian, but compiled from much older sources. The four parts are:

1. The *Codex Justinianus* [*Codex*] - (all of the extant constitutions, going back to the time of Hadrian)
2. The *Pandects* [*Digest*] - (writings of great Roman jurists, along with current edicts. It constituted the current Roman law of the time.)
3. The *Institutiones* [*Institutes*] - (intended as a study guide for law schools, and included extracts from the Codex and Digest.)
4. The *Novellae Constitutiones* - (new laws and statutes adopted during Justinian's time.)

The *Corpus Juris Civilis* is the source of all modern "contract law," as well as various theories of property rights. Again, the approach taken is completely bestial: "The things we take from our enemies become immediately ours by the law of nations, so that even freemen thus become our slaves... Precious stones, gems and other things found upon the seashore become immediately, by natural law, the property of the finder." (*The Institutes; Of Things*)

The argument employed by Hugo Grotius in his work *On the Freedom of the Seas* is entirely based on Roman Law. If you have read Grotius, compare him with the following quotes: "By the law of nature these things are common to mankind -- the air, running water, the sea, and consequently the shores of the sea." And also: "Wild beasts, birds, fish, and all animals... so soon as they are taken by anyone, immediately become by the law of nations the property of the captor; for natural reason gives to the first occupant that which had no previous owner." (both from, *The Institutes; Of Things*)

This issue of Roman Law is not esoterica. Roman Law has defined the oligarchical notion of natural law and jurisprudence down to the modern era. The Napoleonic Code was perhaps the worst modern fascist version of Roman Law, but sadly, the axioms of Roman Law can be found to this day in the constitutions of many nations, including in present-day Europe.

Aristotle

Despite the earlier Platonic (Augustinian) influence over Western Christianity—a Platonic outlook which had influenced the mind and actions of Charlemagne—the Venetian ascendancy of the 12th and 13th centuries brought with it an onslaught of Aristotelianism. This Aristotelean pestilence entered Europe via two routes. First was the revival of Roman Law itself, which is Aristotelean, both in its very nature and due to the fact that many ancient Roman jurists were leading Aristotelean scholars. (The most famous of these was Paulus, circa 200 AD). The second entry point was the translation, and republishing of Aristotle's writings.

This Aristotelean revival began in the 11th century, and

progressed in tandem with the aforementioned developments at Bologna. At first the new translations (into Latin) came from Islamic Spain and northern Africa, and standard histories usually emphasize this. However, after the 1209 Venetian conquest of Constantinople and seizure of Cyprus, it was Venice that became the center of Aristotelean scholarship. The first European translation of Aristotle—his *Politics*—was published there in 1270. This work quickly became the most-studied non-religious text in Europe. The emerging European universities, including the Italian ones, as well as Oxford, Cambridge, and Paris, all became centers of the revived study of Roman Law and Aristotle, such that by the late 13th century, at many of the universities, the three main areas of study were Canon Law, Roman Law, and Aristotle.

After the Turkish conquest of Constantinople in 1453, thousands of Greek emigres fled to Crete, a Venetian possession, creating a second wave of Venetian Aristotelean scholarship.

Why start this way?

Although the post-1582 developments in Venice, Amsterdam, and London ushered in a new modern form of Empire, in a certain sense the peculiarly European characteristics of Empire that have come down to us today, can all be found in the first Venetian empire of the 12th, 13th, and 14th centuries, from the usury of the Venice-dominated Lombard League to the anti-human notions of Aristotelianism and Roman Law. Throughout the ensuing centuries, wherever you find Aristotle and Roman Law, you are certain to find the Venetian pestilence, and vice-versa. No matter what other changes might have occurred, they are always present. Always. No virus, no plague of any kind, has tortured the human species throughout its history, as have these dead ideas from the past.

Nominalists misunderstand everything about history. Thus, historians-without-a-clue will conclude that the Lombard League of cities was deployed against the expansion of the German EMPIRE. Some will even talk about the EMPIRE of Charlemagne. Such analysis is really just drivel. Empires are not empires because of their geographical boundaries, nor because they have hereditary monarchies, nor because they have colonies. Empires are empires because of their species nature, one where humans are treated like cattle, to be used and culled by an oligarchy. As I said, most historians are badly confused; how else could they possibly refer to Venice as a republic?

In historical research, as in tracking a dangerous animal, one looks for the spoor. Roman Law and Aristotelianism are the Empire's spoor.

II. The Venetian Empire, before and after the Council of Florence

Doge Enrico Dandolo: leader of the infamous 4th Crusade

Beginning with the nation-building policies of Charlemagne, and continuing—in a much more uneven way—under the Salic and Hohenstaufen rulers in Germany, Europe began to slowly recover from the devastation of the Roman Empire and its aftermath. By the 12th century, population was increasing, as was food production and manufacturing activity. These positive developments were all destroyed by the policies of Venice, particularly after 1250, as Europe was driven into a collapse, resulting in a horror beyond anything in the imagination of even the worst of the Caesars.

Culturally, unlike the realm of Charlemagne, Venice of the 12th through 14th centuries was very much a product of its Roman and Byzantine past. Never conquered during the Goth invasions, a part of Justinian's empire in the 6th century, and inter-married over centuries with Byzantine nobility, the Venetian oligarchy was never really European, but rather a continuation of the ancient Asian empire model of Babylon and its successors. Through the Venetian Senate, the Council of 10, and the later Council of 3, a form of permanent oligarchy was established, whose power lasted well into the 18th century.

From the period of the first Crusade in 1099 through to the collapse and depopulation of the Black Death in 1347-1351, Europe and the Mediterranean region were dominated by this first manifestation of a Venetian empire. Despite Venice's seizure of Byzantine and other colonies, this was never primarily an empire of geographical expansion, but of maritime and, particularly, financial ascendancy. Unlike Germany, the Low Countries, or France, Venice possessed no industry, save for its giant military/naval factory, the Arsenal. Their power was in their control over trade, particularly trade between Europe and the East, and in banking and currency manipulation.

Venice's first partners in creating their empire were drawn from the Norman nobility of Europe, particularly from France and Angevin England. It was the Normans who acted as the cannon fodder for Venice's wars of conquest, known as the Crusades. Venice also controlled the Black Guelph (Welf) party of the northern Italian cities, allied with the papacy. Beginning with the Guelphs' military campaigns against Frederick Barbarossa in 1176, the Venice-controlled Lombard League was born, a group which came to include all of the major cities of northern Italy, with the exception of Milan. These Lombard League cities then served as the centers for the emergence of the usurious Lombard banking system.

This Venetian-controlled alliance of the northern Angevin/Norman nobility, the Guelph-dominated Lombard League, and the Vatican, ruled over Europe, and through the power of the banking houses of the Lombard League, imposed a financial system based entirely on extreme usury and economic looting. It was also at this time that Venice became the premier slave-trading center of the Mediterranean.

Although 13th century Lombard banking is usually associated with the major Florentine banks of Bardi, Peruzzi, and Acciaiuoli, as has been conclusively documented in other locations,[5] Venice's control of gold and

---

[5] *Money and Banking in Medieval and Renaissance Venice*, by Frederick C. Lane; and "How Venice Rigged the First, and Worst, Global Financial Crash," by Paul Gallagher, *Fidelio*, Vol. 4, No. 4, 1995

silver trading made it the actual "godfather" of the Lombard Banking system of this period.   Not only the Florentine banks, but increasingly every royal court in Europe, from Naples, to France, to England, to Castile, and even including the papal court at Avignon, came under the domination of Venice's control of silver and gold trading.

For more than 100 years, this Venetian-created monstrosity destroyed and looted the continent of Europe. Countries such as Naples and England were driven into bankruptcy; woolen and other production collapsed; food production declined; and, by no later than 1290, Europe began to lose people. Cities, towns, and nations were all ensnared in the Venice-Lombard web of debt and usury. In the absence of sovereign national credit institutions, the Lombard bankers became the *de facto* creditors and financial dictators of Europe.

Much like the financial vultures of today, the Lombard bankers not only drove their victims into debt, but used that debt to seize real assets. By 1325, for example, the Peruzzi bank owned all of the revenues of the Kingdom of Naples, the most productive grain belt of the entire Mediterranean area. In Castile and England the entirety of wool production was pledged as collateral for the Lombard loans. The situation in France, Hungary, and elsewhere was similar. Europe was transformed into a gigantic tax farm as local rulers looted their economies and people to send money across the Alps.

By 1300 whole sections of Europe were experiencing severe economic decline, food shortages, and loss of population. Continent-wide famines struck in 1314-17, and again in 1328-9. The financial bubble began to burst in the 1320s, with a first wave of Lombard banking failures. Financial doomsday arrived in 1342-1345 with the collapse of the Acciaiuoli, Buonacorsi, Bardi, and Peruzzi banking houses.

In 1347, the Black Death arrived, striking a population already in a state of collapse, weakened by famine and disease, as a result of the economic looting of the previous century. The plague swept across Europe from 1347 to 1351 – killing an estimated 30 to 40 percent of the population, and in many areas far more than 50 percent. From 1351 through to the early 15th century, the population declined further, as disease, famine and economic devastation played themselves out.

The Renaissance & the creation of nation states

The horror visited on Europe from 1320 to 1420 destroyed the social fabric as well as the political and philosophical axioms of the medieval world. One result was that, although the Venetian empire survived the collapse of the late 14th century, its power was greatly weakened, giving political leaders throughout Europe the ability to throw off the Lombard financial shackles and begin to rebuild their nations. By the early 1400s, the remaining Lombard bankers were being expelled from country after country: Aragon in 1401, England in 1403, Flanders in 1409, and France in 1410. The Venetian *ultramontane* financial empire crumbled as nations began to exert sovereignty over their own affairs.

At the same time, the profound existential nature of the 14th century catastrophe destroyed the previously hegemonic axioms of the medieval world. By the early 1400s, a sea-change in philosophical and scientific outlook began to emerge, including a re-examination of the nature of Man and his role in the universe.

Beginning with the revival of the works of Dante Alighieri – including not only his *Commedia*, but his political works such as *De Monarchia* – by Giovanni Boccaccio, and continuing into the great breakthroughs of Giotto di Bondone and Filippo Brunelleschi, new ideas in government, science and art began to emerge, ideas coherent with a revolutionary change in Man's self-conception. This process was then intersected by the early 15th century translation and publication of Plato's dialogues.[6]

The greatest figure of this period was the German churchman Nicholas of Cusa. In his writings *On Not-Other* and *On Learned Ignorance*, Cusa refuted the medieval scientific methodology of Aristotle and Euclid, returning science to its Platonic/Pythagorean origin. In *The Catholic Concordance* Cusa established the principle of the *Commonwealth*, a nation state based on the principle of *agapé*, of the Common Good, and in his *On the Peace of Faith*, he presented the basis for an ecumenical peace among nations.

Cusa's life work, almost universally ignored in the history books of today, represents one of the greatest revolutionary interventions in all of human history. In his scientific and mathematical writings, Cusa destroyed Aristotelianism, and returned science to its rightful domain of hypothesis and human creativity. For Cusa, Man was not a beast, a farm animal, or a slave, but each human being was a creature endowed with creative reason. This conception of "man, the creator" is also seen in the great Dome built by Filippo Brunelleschi, constructed on the principle of the catenary, at the Santa Maria del Fiore Cathedral in Florence; as well as in the breakthroughs in dynamics and perspective by Leonardo DaVinci, the map of Toscanelli which provided Columbus with a route to the

---

[6] "The Renaissance and the Rediscovery of Plato and the Greeks," by Torbjorn Jerlerup, *Fidelio*, Vol XII, No.3, 2003

New World, and many, many other radiating effects.

Cusa organized the 1439 Council of Florence, which brought leaders from throughout Europe into an agreement on the *agapic* principle of the *filioque*, and established the basis for a new civilization, built on the principles of human reason, the Common Good, and national sovereignty.

In 1461 Louis XI ascended to the throne of France, and proceeded to establish the first modern sovereign nation-state, based on Cusa's Commonwealth principle.[7] Louis proceeded to build ports, roads, schools, printing houses, industry, and infrastructure. He provided support for the cities, created a national currency, and broke the power of the feudal baronies. These are Louis' own words, taken from his book *Le Rosier des Guerres* (The Rosebush of Wars):

> "Considering that the characteristic of Kings and Princes and their Knights, is that their estate and vocation is to defend the common good, both ecclesiastic and secular, and to uphold justice and peace among their subjects, and to do good, they will have good in this world and in the other and out of doing evil will only come grief; and one must count one day on leaving this world to go and give an account of one's undertakings and receive one's reward. And to expose their lives for others, of which among all other estates of the world is most to be praised and honored. And because the common good which concerns many, which is the public matter of the Realm is more praiseworthy than the particular, by which the common good is often frustrated; we have gladly put in writing the deeds

---

[7] "The Commonwealth of France's Louis XI: Foundations Of The Nation State," by Pierre Beaudry, *New Federalist*, July 3, 1995

of princes and of their knights and all the good tenets that served their cause...."

Read the above quote again, and then compare what Louis says about the Common Good, with the notions of Roman Law and the policies of the Lombard League discussed above. Nicholas of Cusa's discovery of the Commonwealth principle – a discovery of an actual *universal principle* – was one of the most profound revolutions in human history, and it produced a sea-change in the political organization of humanity.

Louis XI's example was contagious. In 1485, Henry Tudor, who had lived in Brittany and France during the reign of Louis, invaded England, overthrew the last of the Venetian-allied Plantagenet kings, Richard III, and established Tudor rule. As king, Henry VII adopted the same methods of national economic development and sovereignty that Louis had pursued in France. Like Louis, he attacked the power of the feudal nobility, and implemented national policies inspired by the principle of the Common Good. As had occurred in France, food production, national income, and population all increased, for the first time in more than a century. These initiatives in sovereignty and nation-building were not limited to France and

Louis XI of France

England, but affected the Iberian peninsula, Flanders, and elsewhere. Taken together with the revolution in science undertaken by Nicholas of Cusa and his allies, a new future for mankind seemed to be at hand. With the success of Columbus' trans-Atlantic voyage in 1492, the chance to annihilate the old feudal oligarchic order was unfolding. As Desiderius Erasmus declared to Thomas More in a 1499 letter, humanity seemed poised at the dawn of a "new era."

Venice against the Commonwealth

Erasmus was not wrong in his assessment. The establishing of sovereign nation-states in France and England, together with the radiating influence of Cusa's revolution in science, threatened the very existence of the Venetian system of usury and slavery. But the Venetians fought back.

Demonstrating the same oligarchical arrogance as that of the Olympian gods, the first reaction of Venice to these revolutionary changes was to try to force the genie back in the bottle, to reimpose the feudal world of usury and Aristotle by force and bloodshed. And Venice still possessed the means to try. In the mid-fifteenth century Venice was still the most powerful maritime nation in Europe, controlled Europe's slave and bullion trade, maintained the most extensive political intelligence operations on the continent, and was the home of the most influential center of Aristotelean scholarship in Europe, the University of Padua. Venetian influence over the Vatican was also of paramount importance.

To this end Venice turned to a new ally, the Hapsburg dynasty, first in Austria, then in Spain. As part of this Hapsburg operation, the Venetians created a new financial front to replace that of the defunct Lombard bankers – the

House of Fugger. Jacob Fugger, an insignificant Austrian spice trader residing in Venice, was picked up by the Venetians and made their agent in control of most of the silver and copper mines in central Europe. From the vast wealth accumulated in these operations, Fugger created the most powerful banking house in Europe, and then bankrolled the Austrian Hapsburgs, previously only second-tier German nobility, into control of the Holy Roman Empire.

In 1518, utilizing a series of dynastic marriages, the Hapsburgs took control of Spain, and the Fuggers became also the bankers to the Spanish monarchy. After the Spanish bankruptcy of 1575, the Fuggers were replaced as the financial controllers of the Spanish crown by Venice's junior partner, Genoa. But for Venice, that just meant substituting one proxy for another.[8]

In essence, the 14th century Black Guelph party was reborn as the Holy Alliance, a Venice-Hapsburg-Vatican axis, with Venice in direct control of the Papal Curia. Venice also controlled the policies of Spain through its Fugger and Genoese allies, who, as the creditors to the Spanish government, drained off all of the loot from Spain's massive traffic in gold, silver, and slaves, manipulated every aspect of Spanish policy, and drove the Spanish Crown into bankruptcy several times.

At the same time, Venice launched an all-out counterattack against the revolution in science initiated by Nicholas of Cusa and his followers. Like Zeus they thought they could outlaw man's access to fire through the use of imperial force. This effort culminated in the 1545-1563 Council of Trent, which attempted to reimpose Aristotelean

---

[8] Genoa had been subservient to Venice ever since her defeat by Venice in the 1380 Battle of Chioggia. Previously, although putatively a rival to Venice, Genoa was also a loyal member of Venice's Lombard League syndicate.

rigidity, essentially by Papal decree. The mastermind of this so-called "Catholic Counter-Reformation" was the Venetian Cardinal Gasparo Contarini.

At the heart of this Venetian counteroffensive was the use of terror. Sheer barbaric terror. With the initiation of the Spanish Inquisition in 1478, under the direction of Tomás de Torquemada, Europe was drenched in bloodshed, setting off the Wars of Religion which did not end until 1648. Waves of mass killings, persecution, and inflamed passions engulfed Europe, the victim of which was the

Torquemada's Inquisitors

humanist ideals of the Renaissance.[9] The ensuing decades of partisan religious warfare, creating almost a continent-wide psychosis, were a hammer, aimed at shattering the

---

[9] "Two poor creatures have been burnt, and the whole city has turned Lutheran... Either I am blind or they aim at something else than Luther. They are preparing to conquer the phalanx of the muses." - in a letter from Erasmus to Thomas More, 1523

development of sovereign nation-state commonwealths.[10]

The end of the Old Regime

Ultimately, this Venetian strategy didn't work. By the early 16th century the geopolitical crisis facing Venice was an inescapable reality. The war of the League of Cambrai, from 1509 to 1513, when foreign troops entered the Venetian Lagoon, had exposed the military vulnerability of Venice's defenses. In addition, by mid-century, Venice was threatened with the loss of not only her colonies, but her entire access to trade with the east, at the hands of the Ottoman Turks. Despite the Venetian-Hapsburg-Papal victory at the 1571 Battle of Lepanto, Venice lost Cyprus and other colonies, and was forced to sign a humiliating treaty with the Turks in 1573. Economically, Venice began to hemorrhage. Between 1560 and 1600, the size of the Venetian merchant marine shrank by one half. In 1560 a banking crisis struck, lasting into the 1580s. This was a total collapse, such that by 1584 every private banking house in Venice had closed.

At the same time, the explosion of trans-oceanic travel had created an entirely new strategic reality. Small but significant numbers of Europeans began to emigrate, particularly to the Western Hemisphere, hoping to escape the old world oligarchical matrix. Venice was in no position to meet this challenge of the New World, to undertake the task of imposing a global maritime empire.

Perhaps, if Venice had stuck to its reactionary methods, it could have found a way to overcome its difficulties and deal with most of the challenges mentioned above. But there was one problem that could not be solved using the old medieval methods. The idea of the *Commonwealth* –

---

[10] To understand the face of this evil, see Friedrich Schiller's *Don Carlos*

together with unprecedented scientific and technological progress – had been unleashed by the Renaissance. The zero-growth world of feudalism was forever dead. Despite all of the Venetian-instigated bloodshed and intrigues, human progress was on the march, and some in Venice realized that the new ideas of scientific progress and national sovereignty could not be stopped by the Spanish Inquisitor's torture chamber.

After 1513, new initiatives were taken to transform fundamental features of the Empire, to change it in order to save it. A new direction was required. This all played out over a period of several decades, with important inputs from Italy, Flanders, Spain, and elsewhere. Most importantly, by the time of Martin Luther's confrontation with the Holy Roman Emperor Charles V, at the Diet of Worms in 1521, a faction of the Venetian aristocracy acted to jettison Venice's alliance with Rome and the Hapsburgs, and, instead, to cultivate Venetian influence in the Protestant north.[11] This scenario unfolded over the course of the 16th century. Some within the Venetian oligarchy opposed this new orientation. Ultimately, the creation of a new model of Empire, and the transference of that modern oligarchical system to the north, would have to come from a new leadership in Venice itself.

---

[11] See, e.g., the role of Francesco Zorzi in effecting the English Henry VIII's break with Rome, as well as the activities of Pietro Pomponazzi

III.   The Giovani Revolution

The Bank of Venice

"The modern European civilization unleashed by the Fifteenth-Century "golden" Renaissance, had brought the modern sovereign form of republic, also known as a system of commonwealths, into being. Sarpi's view was that this new enemy, the commonwealth, could not be defeated if the financier-oligarchical interest typified by medieval Venetian usury, refused to adapt to reforms in favor of some limited use of the new ideas of practice associated with the scientific revolution which had been launched, largely, by Venice's chosen chief enemy, Cardinal Nicholas of Cusa."

Lyndon H. LaRouche Jr., "The End of Our Delusion"

In 1613, at the request of the Venetian Senate, the monk Paolo Sarpi (1552-1623), wrote *The History of the Inquisition.* This was followed three years later by Sarpi's most famous work, *The History of the Council of Trent.* With these two writings, issued at a time when he was the chief counselor to the Venetian government, Sarpi officially announced to the world that the Venetian-Spanish-Vatican "Holy" alliance was dead. However, these works only proclaimed what everyone already knew. Earlier, in 1606 , Sarpi had led the Venetian government into an open confrontation with Rome over Papal insistence of ecclesiastical rights in Venice. At the height of the ensuing crisis, Pope Paul V issued a Papal Bull, excommunicating the Venetian Doge, the Senate and every inhabitant of Venice. Shortly thereafter he issued a separate Bull personally excommunicating Sarpi a second time. In addition, he declared a Papal Interdict against the entire state of Venice which remained in effect until 1609. When Venice refused to back down, Rome deployed paid assassins to Venice, where they attacked Sarpi, stabbing him repeatedly in the neck and head and leaving him for dead. Sarpi recovered from his wounds, and from then on Venice never strayed from its new course.

Who were the Giovani?

In the late 1570s, a faction emerged in Venice, determined to move Venice in a new direction. They were named the party of the Giovani (the "youthful"), and in 1582 they broke the power of the Council of 10, and forced the Venetian oligarchy to return political control to the Senate, which the Giovani controlled. These were not downtrodden *sans-culotte* revolutionaries. They came from some of the most powerful oligarchical families in Venice, and their ranks included several future Doges, including Leonardo Donato, who protected Sarpi during the Interdict crisis, and Nicolo Contarini, who was perhaps Sarpi's closest ally among the Venetian nobility.

By the 1590s, it was Sarpi who was the acknowledged intellectual leader of the Giovani faction, and it was Sarpi's views which would determine the strategic policies of Venice until years after his death. Despite the fact that Sarpi and his allies would ultimately move Venice into an open strategic and military alliance with the Protestant north, the actions of the Giovani had nothing to do with religion.

Theirs was a shared goal to save the *system of Empire* which Venice had epitomized for more than four centuries.

The Venetian collaborators of Sarpi were grouped around a series of *ridotti* (salons), but it was the *ridotto* of Andrea Morosini, whose family had contributed numerous Doges to Venice over the centuries, which became the epicenter of Sarpi's inner circle. Participants – other than Sarpi himself – included Giovanni Francesco Sagredo (later to be Sarpi's hands-on controller of Galileo; two of his grandsons would also become Doges), Nicolo Contarini (future Doge and the protector of Monteverdi), Andrea Morosini, Leonardo Donato (another future Doge), Marc Tevisiano, Ottavio Buono, Domenico Molino (he served as Sarpi's go-between in a correspondence with Francis Bacon), Antonio Quirini (one of several members of the Venetian Senate active in the *Ridotto Morosini*, Quirini would publish pamphlets in defense of Sarpi that were placed on the Papal Index), Marini Zane, Leonardo Mocenigo (later the Bishop of Ceneda), Jacopo Morosini, and others.

There were other *ridotti* for other purposes; some were centers of discussions in mathematics, or physiology, such as the *Ridotto Nave d'Oro*, where Galileo spent much of his time when he was not at Morosini's *Ridotto*. Other *ridotti*, like the Paduan home of the Genoese Gian Vincenzo Pinella, were places where Sarpi could make contact with his foreign, particularly Protestant, allies, such as the French Huguenot DuPlessis-Mornay.

Much like the later notorious activities of Madame de Staal, these salons were not either simply social clubs, nor artistic literary groups. On the one hand, Sarpi was the unquestioned leader of the network, and from these *ridotti*, he would launch the creation of his "new science" of empiricism. At the same time, these meeting-places represented the headquarters for a political effort to remake

Venice, and to change the entire geopolitical map of Europe.

The new banking paradigm

Five years after the 1582 Giovani takeover, the first "public" bank in Venice was established, the justly famous *Banco della Piazza di Rialto*, sometimes simply called the Bank of Venice. This was followed, in 1619, by a second bank, the *Banco Giro*, which gradually absorbed the former.

This banking revolution was the Giovani's answer to the Renaissance threat of the sovereign Commonwealth. Under this new banking system, all of the pre-1400 usurious practices of the Lombard bankers were retained, but, essentially, rather than have private family banks loan money to the state, the innovation was to have the financial oligarchy simply take over the state, i.e., to eradicate any principle of national sovereignty, to eliminate the idea of the Common Good, and to make the state itself an arm of the financial oligarchy. *That, in essence, is the core principle of what would become the Anglo-Dutch financial system.*

A recent, interesting, if flawed, paper by the historians Fratianni and Spinelli, which examines both the Venetian banking revolution, as well as the related creation of the *Casa di San Giorgio* in Genoa, provides useful insights into these developments.[12] The mistake Fratianni and Spinelli make is that, in comparing the so-called "public" vs. "private" nature of the banks in Venice and Genoa, they fail to see that the founding of both banks represented an expansion of the power of the financial oligarchy over the civil state, and they try too hard to prove a difference between the Genoese and Venetian experiences. The Bank of Venice and the Casa di San Giorgio were merely first

---

[12] "Did Genoa and Venice Kick a Financial Revolution in the Quattrocento?", by Michele Fratianni & Franco Spinelli, *Oesterreichische Nationalbank*

steps towards a new banking paradigm, and their later emulators in Amsterdam and London would go much further in creating an entirely new form of financial empire.

The Bank of Venice became the direct inspiration for the 1609 Bank of Amsterdam, and together, these two banks were the model for the Bank of England in 1694. People writing at that time were very aware, and very explicit, that the new financial model was derived from Venice. Thus, in the years preceding the 1688 "Glorious Revolution" in England, we find the 1651 proposal by Sir Balthazer Gerbier for the creation of a "bank of payment in London after the style of either the bank of Amsterdam, or that of Venice;" the 1678 book by Dr. Mark Lewis, *Proposals to the King and Parliament*, where he calls for the creation of a national "bank of issuance," based on the design of the Bank of Venice, which he praises as "the perfect credit bank;" and the 1690 call by Nicholas Barbon for the creation of a national public bank, modeled on those "in Venice and Amsterdam." It is therefore, no exaggeration to say that the 1582 Giovani Revolution was the point of origin for the Anglo-Dutch System.

The banking changes in Venice might appear at first as merely a few changes in financial structures and practices, but the axiomatic change was profound. First off, both the *Banco della Piazza di Rialto*, and the subsequent *Banco Giro* were granted a monopoly by the Venetian government on the issuance of bank notes and bills of credit. The notes of these banks were declared legal tender by the Venetian government, and they circulated publicly as the legal equivalent of money. Although both the Venice bank, as well as the *San Giorgio* in Genoa, also functioned as deposit banks, taking in deposits, making loans, and conducting specie transactions, it was this change in their relation to the state which was key.

This was the new paradigm, from which everything later developed. As a consequence of the massive new financial resources at its disposal, during this period Venice made the shift from a commercial economy to primarily a rentier and speculative economy. By 1620, Venice had become the foremost European center as a clearinghouse for Bills of Exchange.

For the oligarchical *fondi*, it is not the individual Venetian, Spanish, Dutch or British empires which are important. Nations are obstacles to the oligarchy. For the *fondi*, it is the *System of Empire* that is fundamental. With the creation of the Banco della Piazza di Rialto, and its later imitators in Amsterdam and London, the oligarchy had invented, not national banks, but the beginnings of what we would call today private *central banking*. The institutions of the state were made subservient, or more accurately, were fused to the private banking system. This, of course, is the essential idea behind the 20th century's "corporativism" of the Mussolini regime, as well as the ideological descendants of Mussolini, like Felix Rohatyn, today. The Commonwealth was to be eliminated, to be supplanted by a world run by the *fondi*.

Moving the Empire to the north

After the assassination of the Dutch leader William the Silent in 1584, the potential for a commonwealth transformation of the Netherlands[13] was eliminated. The Spanish army's destruction of Antwerp in 1585, and the closure of the Antwerp *Bourse* (stock exchange), then led to the "great exodus" from the southern provinces of the Netherlands to the north, with more than 19,000 merchants, bankers, and Bourse speculators fleeing

---

[13] See *The History of the Revolt of the Netherlands,* by Friedrich Schiller

Antwerp, and most settling in Amsterdam. In Amsterdam, the earlier speculative practices of the *Bourse* would be wedded with the new Venetian banking model, to produce a new financial capital for the Empire. The early fruits of this effort came quickly, with the founding of the Dutch East India Company in 1602, the Amsterdam Exchange (the *New Bourse*) in 1608, and the Bank of Amsterdam in 1609. That same year the Giovani-controlled Venetian Senate became the first government in Europe to officially recognize Dutch independence from Spain, and to exchange ambassadors.

Within a few years the financial revolution in Amsterdam would be mimicked in several other locations, including the founding of the Banks of Hamburg and Sweden, and similar events in other northern maritime cities that were previously associated with the Hanseatic League.

Venice's next step in making this shift to the north irreversible, was to pull the Netherlands tighter into the Venetian orbit, while simultaneously initiating a similar transformation in England. The key to this operation was the Venetian confrontation with Rome during the Interdict crisis, and the subsequent role of Venice in provoking the Thirty Years War of 1618-1648.

Sarpi's public leadership during the Interdict, and the failed effort to assassinate him, had the effect of making him, a Roman Catholic monk, the hero of the Protestant world. Sarpi was lionized among political, religious, and intellectual circles in Geneva, Paris, London, Amsterdam, and elsewhere. As news of the Interdict spread through Europe, the first government to officially defend Venice was the Dutch Estates General which offered military aid. The Dutch Stadholder Maurice of Nassau personally tendered his services to Venice. From 1610 to 1618 there existed a state of undeclared war between Venice and Hapsburg

Spain, during which Venice and the Netherlands were in an unofficial military alliance. During the 1615-1617 war between Venice and Hapsburg Austria, 5,000 Dutch troops were sent to serve in Venice, and 12 Dutch warships blockaded the Adriatic to prevent Spanish aid to Austria.

Henry Wotton, the English Ambassador to Venice and a Sarpi sycophant, worked tirelessly during this period, attempting to recruit the English King James I into a military alliance with Venice. He also arranged for the 1618 publication in London of the first English translation of Sarpi's *History of the Council of Trent*. Sarpi's plan was to draw the Dutch, James I of England, and the German Protestant princes into a war against Spain, the Holy Roman Emperor and the Papacy. The ensuing chaos could then be spun back into France, rekindling her religious wars after the 1610 assassination of King Henry IV. In the process, the heritage of Louis XI's and Henry VII's commonwealths would be eradicated, and new clones of Venice would be consolidated in London and Amsterdam.

The role of Sarpi and his agents in manipulating events leading up to the outbreak of war in 1618 is well documented in several locations. For example, it was Sarpi, personally, who advised Christian, the Prince of Anhalt, and his advisor Christoph von Dohna, to induce Frederick V, the Elector of Palatine, to accept the throne of Bohemia, the event which actually triggered the outbreak of hostilities. Meanwhile, the Venetian ally Maurice of Nassau, from his court in The Hague, encouraged both the Bohemians and the same Elector of Palatine into open revolt against the Hapsburgs, and he provided financial aid (100,000 *guilders* per month), as well as weapons and ammunition, which were shipped from the United Provinces to Frederick's army in Bohemia.

At the same time, Sarpi dispatched his personal

assistant Fulgenzio Micanzio to London to plead with King James to intervene militarily, and Sarpi's agent, the English Ambassador Henry Wotton, went to Vienna, where he conducted secret communications with Elizabeth, the wife of the Elector of Palatine. Elizabeth also happened to be the daughter of James I, and Sarpi and Wotton hoped that King James could be induced to enter the war in defense of his daughter.

The foolish Elector Frederick took Sarpi's bait. He accepted the Bohemian throne, thus setting off the war which Sarpi wanted. Frederick (known as the "Winter King") was quickly defeated by the Austrian army, and lost not only Bohemia but the Palatine as well, ending his days as a political refugee at the Orange Court in The Hague.

But the war produced exactly the effect Venice desired. The old Rome-Hapsburg domination of Europe, a domination which Venice had earlier done so much to create, was broken. The Venetian-Calvinist alliance gave Venice an entry-point to spread its influence and methods northward; the power of the Venetian Party in London, grouped around Robert Cecil, Francis Bacon, and the Cavendish family was greatly enhanced; and the Netherlands were firmly within Venice's grip.

In 1618, acting as the official *Consultore* of the Venetian government, Sarpi personally directed the signing of the Dutch-Venetian alliance. It included a mutual defense pact against the Hapsburgs, and when the Dutch resumed direct war against the Spanish in 1621, the Venetians supplied the Dutch government at The Hague with more than 1 million *ducats* towards the war effort.

IV. Sarpi's Web

FRA PAOLO SARPI.

"Will you walk into my parlor?" said the spider to the fly;

"Tis the prettiest little parlor that ever you may spy.
The way into my parlor is up a winding stair,
And I have many curious things to show when you are there."

"Oh no, no," said the little fly; "to ask me is in vain,
For who goes up your winding stair can ne'er come down again."
— Mary Howitt

In 1598, Sir Edwin Sandys, then residing in Venice, wrote a book on the state of religion in Europe, titled *Europae Speculum*. Sandys' editor, and alleged co-author was Paolo Sarpi, who had befriended Sandys during the latter's extended stay in Venice. In 1605 Sandy's book was published, in Paris, by Sarpi's friend and confident, the Huguenot leader Giovanni Diodoti, complete with an introduction supplied by Sarpi himself.

Nine years after leaving Venice, Sandys became one of the founders of the London Virginia Company, chartered by King James I, for the purpose of establishing English colonies in North America. In 1618, Sandys was made treasurer of the company and effectively ran it until 1623. In 1619, under Sandys leadership, two dozen African slaves, purchased from a Dutch man-of-war, were brought into Virginia, the first black slaves in an English-speaking

North American colony. The economy of the colony was organized around a series of plantations, including "Captain Lawne's Plantation" and "Captain Warde's Plantation," and it was Sandys who also introduced the cultivation of tobacco as the major cash crop of the colony. Thus was the tidewater slave-plantation system established, and the seedling of the later Confederate States of America planted on North American soil. Sandys later sat in Parliament for many years where he introduced a number bills supporting free trade, and was active in the affairs of the British East India Company until his death.

The above snapshot of the Sarpi/Sandys relationship is given to illustrate the breadth of Sarpi's influence and reach in the years from 1582 to 1623. The intent here is not to establish Sarpi as a conspiratorial mastermind, but rather to emphasize that he was at the center of the growing network of individuals who were determined to bring into existence new forms of imperial rule. Additionally, Sarpi's methodology in science and mathematics – in violent opposition to the Platonic approach of Nicholas of Cusa in physical science – had far-reaching effects. His contacts, correspondence, and networks (not including his personal coterie in the *ridotti* of Venice), were staggeringly widespread. His web of followers included intimates in most of the courts of Europe, leading scientific circles, and the major universities, including Geneva, Leyden, Oxford and Cambridge. His correspondence was voluminous. Despite the fact that most of Sarpi's personal papers were destroyed by fire in 1769, there are 430 letters from Sarpi still extant. During the period of the Interdict and later, Sarpi had unrestricted access to all of the dispatches sent from abroad by Venice's Ambassadors,[14] placing him at the center of

---

[14] *News Networks in 17th Century Britain and Europe,* by Joan Raymond, Routledge Press, 2006

Venetian intelligence-gathering operations. His letters contain references to events as widespread as the Spanish gold trade, movements of the Dutch fleet, political changes in Egypt and Persia, and the issue of colonization of the Americas. And, of course, there is also the scientific and philosophical correspondence.

The effect of the personal acclaim which descended on Sarpi, as a result of his role during the Interdict, cannot be underestimated. Not only was his name on the tongues of the elite throughout Europe, many young aspiring aristocrats actually traveled to Venice to meet the great man himself, including the future British Prime Minister Robert Cecil, another founder of the London Virginia Company William Cavendish, and the "philosopher" Thomas Hobbes.

It is impossible to fully analyze the entire Sarpi network, but I will use the rest of this chapter to give thumbnail profiles of about a dozen of Sarpi's allies and disciples. The truth is there were dozens of such Sarpi allies, but these few brief sketches will hopefully give some indication of the scope and nature of Sarpi's reach.

Henry Wotton – The only man ever to serve three times as the British Ambassador to Venice (1604-1612, 1616-1619, 1621-1624), Wotton was Sarpi's staunchest political supporter within the British aristocracy. It is likely he met Sarpi as early as 1590, during a visit to Venice, and it is certain that in 1593 he was living at the home of Sarpi confident Isaac Casaubon in Geneva. From 1604 to 1608, Sarpi and Wotton met constantly with the Venetian Senate during the Interdict crisis, and during this period Wotton was under the personal protection of the Giovani Doge Leonardo Donato.

Wotton also played an important role in recruiting and

organizing the pro-Venetian circle at Oxford University, grouped around the Italian Protestant Albericus Gentili. Among others, this group included Robert Cecil, Thomas Walsingham, John Donne, and James Florio. When Galileo's *Sidereus Nuncias* (Starry Messenger) was published in Venice in 1610, Wotton sent a copy to Robert Cecil on the very same day.

Francis Bacon – Bacon was brought into contact with Sarpi by William Cavendish, shortly after Cavendish's protégé Thomas Hobbes began serving as Bacon's personal secretary. Cavendish was in regular contact with Sarpi, and

there are indications that Hobbes' appointment may have been arranged at the suggestion of Sarpi or his aide Micanzio. In 1616 Cavendish personally initiated the correspondence between Sarpi and Bacon, which then lasted for many years. In the course of their relationship, Bacon sent many of his works, including his *Essays*, to Sarpi for critique,

and he looked to Sarpi as his philosophical and scientific mentor. Micanzio, in one of his letters to William Cavendish, said of Bacon, "that he is so full of knowledge, moral and divine, that the abundance of this breast is communicated to whatsoever he reads."

Micanzio actually became Bacon's official literary agent

in Venice, helping to spread his fame there, and another Sarpi ally, Marco Antonio de Dominis, also aided Bacon by translating his *Essays* into Italian.

Bacon's famous philosophical *method of induction, where understanding proceeds from the senses to the intellect*, is taken entirely from Sarpi, as is easily demonstrated by comparing it with Sarpi's *Pensieri #146*, written many years earlier.[15] Bacon was, in fact the perfect agent for spreading Sarpi's method of empiricism into England, and his philosophical influence continued to grow in the years following his death in 1626, culminating in the founding of the Oxford Group (Invisible College) in the 1640s, the forerunner of the British Royal Society.

Phillippe du Plessis-Mornay – A major Calvinist leader, and the reputed author of the "monarchomach"[16] *Vindiciae*

contra Tyrannos, Mornay was sometimes referred to as the "Huguenot Pope." A graduate of the Venetian-controlled University of Padua, Mornay was an intimate associate of Paolo Sarpi. He made many visits to the *ridotti* of Venice, and he was at Sarpi's side throughout the Interdict crisis. Mornay was also a close friend of the English aristocrat Philip Sidney, and visited Sidney at his home in Penshurst. Sidney translated Mornay's *A Work Concerning the Trueness of the Christian Religion* into English, and after Sidney's death, his wife Mary published her own translation of another work by Mornay, *A Discourse of Life and Death,*

---

¹⁵ See footnote #23
¹⁶ See Chapter 6

as well as two original poems in praise of Mornay.

Mornay was also a leading advisor to Henry of Navarre, and according to some sources rivaled even Sully in influence. After Henry's conversion to Catholicism in 1593, Mornay resigned from his service. He then established the most influential Huguenot school in Europe, the University of Saumur, which became his base of operations for the remainder of his life.

Francois Hotman - a French lawyer, Hotman lived in Geneva from 1547 to 1556, working as Jean Calvin's secretary, and accompanying Calvin to the Diet of Worms. In 1560, Hotman was one of the principal organizers of the failed Amboise conspiracy (a Huguenot plot to overthrow the Guise family, and put Louis I Bourbon, the Prince of Conde, on the French throne). From 1560 to 1572 Hotman was a principal leader of the Huguenots. In 1572 he published his major work *Franco-Gallia*, in which he attacked the power of the monarchy. Hotman was both a friend and years-long correspondent of Paolo Sarpi. He also maintained a lengthy correspondence with Alberico Gentili at Oxford.

Marcantun (Marco Antonio) de Dominis – a leading mathematics and Theology professor at the University of Padua, de Dominis was for many years on intimate terms with Sarpi. At Padua he conducted experiments on optics, physics, and mechanics, utilizing Sarpi's new empiricist methodology. A Roman Catholic Bishop, de Dominis sided with Venice during the Interdict. To escape the Inquisition, he fled to Geneva in 1615, and two years later Henry Wotton arranged for his departure for England. By 1617 he was lecturing in Cambridge, and in 1619 he was named Dean of Windsor College. Before leaving Venice, de Dominis was given a copy of the *History of the Council of Trent* by Sarpi, which with Wotton's help, de Dominis then had published in London.

De Dominis was a key entry-point for Sarpi into British scientific circles. Based on earlier work by Sarpi, de Dominis developed a theory of the tides, that was later  incorporated into Isaac Newton's theory of gravitation. In 1611 he published a book on optics which was also highly praised by Newton. De Dominis also played an important role in the "handling" of Francis Bacon, including translating Bacon's *Essays* into Italian, and arranging to have them published in Venice.

Eventually, de Dominis met a very sad end. Under threats from the Vatican, he returned to Rome and attempted to rejoin the Catholic Church, but he was arrested for his previous heresy. He died in prison awaiting trial. By order of the Inquisition, his body was dragged through the streets of Rome, and then publicly burned.

Huig de Groot (Hugo Grotius) – Arguably, one of the most influential writers on the subject of international law in the last 400 years, Grotius was very much ensnared in Sarpi's web. Much of Grotius' theories on law and trade are actually taken wholesale from the theorists of the Spanish School of Salamanca,[17] and it was the Salamancans' pluralist free-market views on international law which were incorporated, almost in toto, in Grotius' work *De Jure Praedae*, which, in turn, served as the philosophical justification for the new Amsterdam-based system of

---

[17] See Chapter 7

Empire.

Grotius was for many years in correspondence with Sarpi, and his attitude can only be described as groveling. He referred to Sarpi as "Paolo the Great," and looked to

Sarpi for approval of his works. Unfortunately for Grotius, from Sarpi's standpoint, both he and Oldenbarneveldt were on the wrong side of the political fight in the Netherlands, which reached a climax in 1618. Sarpi supported Grotius' enemies in the House of Orange, not for ideological reasons, but because they were the "war party," committed to a Dutch military alliance with Venice and bringing the Dutch into the hostilities against the Hapsburgs. When Grotius and Oldenbarneveldt were arrested, Sarpi shed no tears.

Later, in exile in Paris, Grotius would return to the Sarpi fold and become an active member of the empiricist Mersenne Circle, which included Thomas Hobbes and members of the Cavendish family, and was run directly out of Venice by Sarpi's secretary Micanzio.

Giovanni Diodati - Born in Geneva, Diodati became the third head of the Geneva Church, succeeding Theodore Beza, who was the successor to Jean Calvin. In 1618, he was one of the leaders of the Synod of Dort, which helped bring Venice's ally, Maurice of Nassau, into power in the Netherlands. In 1607, Diodoti was brought to Venice by du Plessis-Mornay, and some reports of the period suggest that, during the Interdict, it was a triumvirate of Sarpi,

Diodoti, and William Bedell (Henry Wotton's chaplain), which effectively ran the Venetian government. Diodoti was eventually frustrated in his goal to bring Venice into the Calvinist fold. He failed to see that this was not Sarpi's aim. Sarpi was no Protestant.[18] Sarpi's relations with the Calvinists, were in fact, like those of the spider to the fly. They may be inhabiting the same web, but their purposes for being there are quite different.

Diodati also translated into French, and had published in Paris, both Sarpi's *History of the Council of Trent,* and Edwin Sandys' *Europae Speculum.*

Isaac Casaubon - Born in Geneva to French Huguenot parents, Casaubon became a professor of Greek studies at Calvin's Geneva Academy in 1581. He maintained extensive contacts with leading academic circles throughout Europe, and it was through him that Sarpi frequently passed letters, particularly to his networks at the University of Leyden in the Netherlands. Casaubon's Geneva home functioned as a way-station for many travelers on their way to Venice. Casaubon was also a close collaborator of Joseph Scaliger, the patron of Grotius in Leyden. He later moved to France, but in 1610, after the assassination of Henry IV, he fled to England in the company of Lord Wotton of Marley (the brother of Henry Wotton, and a member of James I's Privy Council). In England he entered into the personal service of King James I. Throughout his life he maintained a

---

[18] *Paolo Sarpi: Between Renaissance and Enlightenment,* by David Wooten, Cambridge, 1983

regular correspondence with Sarpi.

Thomas Hobbes and William Cavendish – the story of Thomas Hobbes and the Cavendish family will be told later in this work.[19] For now I will just say that the Cavendish family were unquestionably the closest personal allies that Sarpi had in England. William Cavendish, the Second Earl

Thomas Hobbes

of Devonshire, accompanied Thomas Hobbes on a trip to Venice in 1614, where they both met with Paolo Sarpi and his associates.[20] Following this trip, Cavendish maintained a 13 year correspondence with Sarpi and his secretary Micanzio, from 1615 to 1628. Seventy-seven of Sarpi's letters from this correspondence still exist, all translated from the Italian into English by Thomas Hobbes. It was thought for many years that Micanzio wrote the letters, but it is now proven that, until the time of his death in 1623, Sarpi himself was the author.[21]

It was also this same Cavendish who was a founding Director of the Virginia Company, and a member of the group which seized control of the Company in 1619. His allies at the Company, and in Parliament, included Southampton, Edwin Sandys, John Danvers, and several others. During his tenure as a Director of the Virginia Company, Cavendish gave one of his shares to Hobbes,

---

[19] See Chapter 6
[20] This is confirmed in a letter written by the then British Ambassador to Venice, Dudley Carleton.
[21] Joan Raymond, op. cit.

allowing Hobbes to attend Directors' meetings.

Thomas Hobbes later became active in the Micanzio-run Paris-based Mersenne Circle, which was to become a center for the propagation of Galileo's works, and a hotbed for empiricist science. It was during the Mersenne Circle period that Hobbes would write *The Leviathan* and *De Cive*, his recipes for oligarchical rule.

William of Ockham

V. Empiricism against the Renaissance

"What has philosophy to do with measuring. It's the mathematicians you've got to trust; they are the surveyors of empty air the way I can survey the field and tell you how long it is."

Le Opere di Galileo Galilei (The Works of Galileo Galilei)

A necessary preface to this chapter is required here. Some readers who are expecting a chronological recitation which focuses on the military, banking and related aspects of Empire may grow impatient with an extended discussion which delves into the realms of philosophy, science and even metaphysics. That would be a mistake.

As stated earlier, empires are not empires because of their form, but rather, it is to their axiomatic nature, their view of Man, that one must look, in order to understand the issue at hand. The Oligarchical Principle rests on a view of Man absolutely hostile to the outlook of Dante, Nicholas of Cusa and Cusa's allies and successors. And, it was Sarpi's bestial view of Man that we see later realized in the mature liberal British Empire of Adam Smith, Parson Malthus, Jeremy Bentham, John Stuart Mill, the Huxley's, H.G Wells and Bertrand Russell. The Gouverneur Morris-authored *Preamble* to the United States Constitution was a declaration of war against precisely that oligarchical outlook.

Don't just look at the policies; peer behind the curtain to the *outlook* from whence the policies derive.

Venice's break with the Holy Alliance was not simply political; it was a realization by Sarpi and his associates that feudalism and backwardness could no longer be imposed by brute force and superstition. The Renaissance idea of the Commonwealth, Cusa's revolution in physical science, and the economic progress they both engendered, could no longer be contained either by Venice's purely geopolitical maneuvering, nor by the belief structures of the middle ages. These beliefs were, in fact, inevitably doomed. The work of Cusa, leading a century later into the revolutionary discoveries of Johannes Kepler, annihilated the entire medieval Aristotelean philosophy.

Sarpi knew that there was no saving the old mechanisms of social control. In order to preserve oligarchical rule he formulated a threefold strategy: 1) Develop a new science of radical materialism, known as *empiricism*, and demand that all scientific investigation utilize this empirical method; 2) Use the "discoveries" of this new empirical science, to falsely claim for himself and his associates the laurels for overturning the dictatorship of Aristotelianism (this is where the "Galileo Project" fits in);[22] 3) Utilize sympathetic networks and individuals, to spread this new empirical science from one corner of Europe to another, until it was hegemonic everywhere.

Lyndon LaRouche has defined the empirical method of Sarpi as follows:

---

[22] The success of this aspect of Sarpi's plan can be seen today in the widespread belief, regularly taught in universities, that the empirical approach of Galileo, Newton and Descartes was a lawful outgrowth of the Renaissance, where, in reality, it was the opposite of everything Brunelleschi, Cusa, Da Vinci, and Kepler were trying to develop.

- "First, the empiricist assumes that no experimentally verifiable knowledge exists outside the bounds of simple sense-certainty.

- "Secondly, therefore, every cause-effect relationship which can not be located explicitly in a sense-observed agency, is related to a domain of such forms of attributed bias in statistical behavior of observable events, or to some anonymous agency to which neither sense-certainty nor cognitive reason provides access.

- "Thirdly, the second element leaves available a niche for creating the illusion of the existence of purely magical spiritual powers, operating entirely outside the reach of access by sense-certainty, but able to make arbitrary interventions, even capriciously, into the domain of sense-certainty."[23]

Essentially what Sarpi did was to say, "Since scientific progress can no longer be stopped, I will determine the method of all future scientific investigation! I will determine, not merely what people think about the physical universe, but *how they think*, and I will ensure that individual human creativity, and the method of lawful hypothesis, as developed by Plato, is banned from all scientific investigation."

In Sarpi's world, there is no hypothesis, there is no creativity, and there is no discovery. Only "observation" and calculation of linear data exists. The 21st century name for this is information theory, and in a world governed by this theory, no human identity is possible. Machines and computers may exist, but the ability to make actual

---

[23] "Laputa's President Bush," by Lyndon H. LaRouche Jr., *Executive Intelligence Review*, May 10, 2002

discoveries of principle has been outlawed. If this seems too difficult to understand, think of the difference between Kepler and Galileo: Kepler sought to discover the *principles* behind astronomical phenomena; Galileo looked at the stars and wrote down his statistical observations. For Galileo, and Sarpi, Kepler's *universal principles* simply do not exist, because they can not be touched, heard, smelled or visibly seen.

To repeat, if you do not come to grips with this issue of the Human Mind, the actual Human Identity, you will never understand the difference between Empire and Republic. It is not simply a question of "who is in charge?". Human beings are not mere animals. It is the Promethean identity of "the Discoverer" which defines the Human Identity, and that is what Sarpi sought to eradicate.

Sarpi & Ockham

In order to develop his new science, Sarpi went back to the writings of a 14th century Franciscan friar named William of Ockham (or Occam). Today Ockham is mostly remembered from just one famous quote, which has come to be known as "Ockham's Razor":

> *"Pluralitas non est ponenda sine neccesitate,"*
> or, in English, "Entities should not be multiplied
> unnecessarily."

Roughly, Ockham's meaning is that when confronted with a scientific problem, in which there are several possible solutions or areas of investigation, the answer lies with the simplest and most obvious. This reductionist method denies any role for human reason or hypothesis and rejects any idea of universal principles. Ockham was also a fanatic materialist, claiming that all human knowledge is based solely on sense perception. Utilizing Ockham's approach, whatever shred of causality or human thought, which had existed previously in Aristotelianism, was eliminated entirely.

Paolo Sarpi stated openly that Ockham was the greatest influence on his own scientific outlook. In a letter to the French Huguenot Francois Hotman on July 22, 1608, Sarpi says of Ockham, *"Io l'ho stimato sopra tutti li scolastici,"* which roughly translated is, "I have esteemed him (Ockham) above all the schoolmen."

Beginning in 1578, and continuing for many years, Sarpi began writing his *Pensieri*, a series of works on mathematics, biology, philosophy and religion. Laudatory references to Ockham abound throughout the work. These writings were never published, but were widely circulated to Sarpi's friends in the *ridotti*. Sarpi authored three sets of *Pensieri*, the first on mathematics, philosophy, and physics, the second on medicine and morals, and the third on religion. In the *Pensieri Filosofici* Sarpi argues on the defects in man's nature which make religion and government necessary in order to control man's passions and baser animalistic impulses. This argument anticipates Descartes' later view of a linear mechanistic physical universe, combined with irrational human emotions. The *Pensieri Religione* contains a long attack on Aristotle and on Christian concepts of natural law. Sarpi states that it is impossible for man to know natural law or any universal principles, due both to the limits on human reasoning, as well as the linear mechanistic nature of the universe itself. In the famous *Pensieri* #146,[24] Sarpi is most explicit in his

---

[24] from Paolo Sarpi: *Pensieri* #146—"There are four modes of philosophizing: the first with reason alone, the second with sense alone, the third with reason and then sense, and the fourth beginning with sense and ending with reason. The first

empiricist method, as well as his extreme materialism. There is no reality whatsoever outside the world of sensory experience.

The *Pensieri* were not Ivory Tower speculations. The ideas set forth by Sarpi were immediately put into practice to develop a new experimental science and a new mathematics, based on his reductionist empiricist methodology. According to his 18th century biographer, who examined Sarpi's private papers at the *Library of the Servi* in Venice, Sarpi's papers included many works on geometry, mechanics, hydraulics, pneumatics, optics, astronomy, and acoustics. Sarpi's first major area of research was his 1582-1585 work on anatomy, a subject which he had earlier studied at Padua. Later, as Sarpi's ideas gained influence in various European university faculties, the earliest recruits were among the professors of medicine and mathematics, and, it was in those fields that Sarpi's mechanistic methods spread most quickly.

Among the initial Venetian group which promoted Sarpi's "new science," were Giovanni Francesco Sagredo, Santorio Santorio, and Marc Antonio de Dominis. De Dominis, who we have already met in the previous chapter, was a Professor of Mathematics at the University of Padua, where he conducted experiments on optics, physics, and mechanics. Sagredo, a leading Venetian aristocrat, was also a mathematician, and he was Sarpi's personal "controller" of Galileo. He actually invented the first modern version of a thermometer, which is usually attributed to Galileo. Santorio was the Chair of Theoretical Medicine at

---

is the worst, because from it we know what we would like to be, not what is. The third is bad because we many times distort what is into what we would like, rather than adjusting what we would like to what is. The second is true but crude, permitting us to know little and that rather of things than of their causes. The fourth is the best we can have in this miserable life." (Scritti filosofici e teologici, Bari: Laterza, 1951, Pensiero 146)

the University of Padua. His belief in mechanics was so insane that for 30 years he not only weighed himself every day, but also weighed all the food and fluids he consumed as well as all the urine and feces he emitted. He was celebrated for his empirical methodology.[25] He denied the "essence" of things, insisting on the fundamental mathematical and mechanical nature of things, which could only be discovered through sense perception.

The Assault on Aristotle

Aristotelianism had dominated Europe from the 11th through the early 15th centuries, including in the universities and the Catholic Church. It was never good, but the anti-cognitive, fixed, perfected, universe of Aristotle was perfect for Venice's zero-growth caste system of the medieval centuries. During that period, Aristotle's views on cosmology, music, biology, and economics were accepted with almost the fervor of religious fundamentalism. After the revolution in science effected by Nicholas of Cusa this became impossible.

The question arises: "What's the big deal? Don't Aristotle and Sarpi both base their ideology on sense-perception?" Yes, they do, but in Sarpi, you have this method *in extremis*. It's like the difference between a body-builder in a gym who says "no pain, no gain" and the Marquis de Sade. The concept "pain" takes on a different meaning. With Sarpi, human reasoning – and all causality – ceases to exist entirely. This insanity later became known as empiricism, and it has many, many modern derivatives and offshoots, but they all have the same mother.

In 1604, the Sarpi cabal unleashed an open public war

---

[25] *Weighing the Soul, Scientific Discovery from the Brilliant to the Bizarre,* by Len Fisher

against Aristotelianism and the Aristotelean priesthood at the University of Padua. At the time, Padua was the premier center of Aristotelean scholarship in all of Europe, and had produced the two most renowned teachers of Aristotelean logic during that era, the professors Giacomo Zabarella (1533-1589) and Cesare Cremonini (1550-1631). The opening salvo of this attack was a series of lectures by Galileo Galilei, targeting Aristotle's cosmology, i.e., the notion of the "fixed stars," existing within a static, perfected universe. These lectures were given a sensational PR treatment by the Sarpi network, based on Galileo's alleged recent discovery of the "New Star," (a super-nova, which, in fact, Galileo did not discover). This was no academic debate; it struck at the center of the Aristotelean establishment, and was nothing less than an attempt to overthrow the entirety of medieval scholasticism.

Even still today Giacomo Zabarella is considered the premier representative of 16th century Italian Aristotelianism. After 1564, he became both the Chair in Logic and the Chair in Natural Philosophy at the University of Padua. A rigid Aristotelean, Zabarella, nevertheless, also insisted on the reality of causality, and said that it is the mind of the scientist which carries out the necessary proofs. He was opposed to using mathematical proofs as a way of arriving at truth. Cesare Cremonini, who succeeded to the Chair of Natural Philosophy in 1591, was, more so than Zabarella, an avowed materialist, and like Pomponazzi before him, he denied the immortality of the soul. Nevertheless, he became Galileo's leading critic at the University of Padua. In 1604 Cremonini was the foremost opponent of Galileo's views on the "New Star, and he was quoted by a contemporary source at the time as saying, "the mathematicians adduce the expressed view that it is bad judgment to forsake the senses and go searching for reason" (i.e. cause). In his 1632 *The Dialogue Concerning Two Chief World Systems*, Galileo ridicules Cremonini, portraying him as the buffoonish figure "Simplicio."

This attack on the Aristotelean establishment was the premier task assigned to Galileo by Sarpi. Although, today, many uninformed people somehow think that Galileo was a champion of Copernicanism, Galileo, in fact, was *one of the last astronomers of the period to endorse helio-centrism*, which he did not do until the publication of his 1632 *Dialogue*. From his arrival in Padua in 1592, up until that much later date, all of Galileo's efforts were concentrated on overthrowing Aristotelean scholasticism on behalf of Sarpi's new empiricism.

Kepler

Johannes Kepler

The 1604 Sarpi-led attack on Aristotelianism was not simply an academic exercise. In 1597, Johannes Kepler's *Mysterium Cosmographicum* was published.[26] Upon the completion of this work, Kepler had sent four copies of the book to Padua, one of which ended up in the hands of Galileo, who passed it on to Sarpi. Galileo subsequently wrote to Kepler, and several short notes passed between

---

[26] For the significance of Kepler, please see *Music & Statecraft, How Space Is Organized*, by Lyndon H. LaRouche, Jr.

them.[27] In September, 1597, Kepler sent a longer letter to Galileo suggesting a collaboration between the two. Following this exchange of letters Galileo cut off all communication with Kepler. Outside of Italy, the publication of the *Mysterium* had a powerful impact on the scientific community and led to Kepler's appointment as Imperial Mathematician to the German Emperor in 1601. In Venice, it led to Sarpi's 1603-1604 unleashing of the Galileo Project. Later, after the publication of Kepler's *Astronomia Nova* (New Astronomy) in 1609, Sarpi again responded, this time with the Venetian telescope demonstrations, and the accelerated campaign to sell Galileo as the premier authority on astronomy.

For the layman it may seem difficult to comprehend the threat which Kepler's work posed to Sarpi's designs. But bear in mind: Kepler was a proclaimed self-conscious follower of the scientific method of Nicholas of Cusa.[28] Not only was his methodology directly contrary to Sarpi's empiricism, it represented an axiomatically different view of the human mind, of human nature itself.

For the empiricists, man is only capable of taking in sensory data, and adding, subtracting and manipulating that data in linear ways to arrive at what they call "verifiable" results. This also holds true for Sarpi's views on mathematics, as well as for the universe as a whole. Anyone who accepts that approach, will ultimately be led to the unenviable conclusion that a super-computer is, in fact, equal, or superior, to the human mind (or soon will be). Cusa and Kepler took the contrary view, that science begins where linear analysis breaks down, where contradictions arise, and where the power of human hypothesis leads to

---

[27] "Galileo and Kepler: Their First Two Contacts," by Edward Rosen, *Isis*, Vol. 57, No. 2
[28] Kepler acknowledged his debt to Cusa in his first published work

the discovery, not of more sensory data, but to true discovery of the universal principles which underlie the ordering of the universe. This is seen both in Cusa's discrediting of Euclidean mathematics (in his critique of Archimedes on the "squaring of the circle"), as well as in Kepler's discovery of the musical harmonics which govern the ordering of our solar system.

After the abortive Kepler-Galileo correspondence of 1597, the Venetians broke off all communication with Kepler for 13 years. During this period, they knew that they could not openly attack him due to his position and widespread prestige. Then, after Galileo's demonstration of the telescope and the publication of his *Sidereus Nuncias*, another attempt was made to bring Kepler under Venetian control. In 1610 Galileo sent a long letter to Kepler, soliciting Kepler's endorsement. Kepler responded with the publication of *Dissertatio cum Nuncio Sidereo*, which essentially challenged Galileo to adopt Kepler's scientific method. Following the publication of the *Dissertatio* no further communication between Kepler and Galileo occurred.

Having failed to co-opt or discredit Kepler, Sarpi next moved to destroy him. In 1618 Galileo publicly assailed Kepler's theory on the origin of comets (Kepler was right, and Galileo was wrong), and, following the publication of Kepler's *Harmonices Mundi* (Harmony of the Worlds), Galileo, in 1624, denounced Kepler as a heretic, a very serious charge, actually a not so veiled death threat. It was also during this period, in 1620, that Henry Wotton, the notorious British ally of Sarpi, traveled to Vienna, met with Kepler, and urged him to move to England. Kepler declined this offer to join the stable of Venetian agents in London. Galileo continued his public attacks, ridiculing Kepler's discovery of the elliptical planetary orbits, and dismissing as a "useless fiction" Kepler's idea that the gravitational force of the moon caused the tides. In both instances, of course, Galileo was wrong, and Kepler was right. In his 1632 *The Dialogue Concerning Two Chief World Systems*, Galileo completely ignores Kepler, the universally recognized scientific genius of his age, while calling the ancient fraud Ptolemy one of greatest minds ever to have philosophized about the structure of the universe.

The True Tale of the Telescope[29]

If one had to pick the single event which transformed Galileo into an international celebrity, it was his demonstration of the telescope in 1609. In August of that year, Paolo Sarpi, acting as the official *Consultore* of the Venetian Government, arranged for Galileo Galilei to perform two demonstrations of his telescope: a public demonstration from the tower of St. Mark, and a second, private demonstration for the Doge and the full Venetian Senate. It was this event, combined with the publication of *Sidereus Nuncius* (Starry Messenger) the following year, which established Galileo as the oligarchical standard-bearer for the overthrow of Aristotelean orthodoxy. He was to hold this position for more than 30 years, and, when he was placed on trial for heresy by the Inquisition in 1633, he was virtually immortalized as a champion of scientific truth.

During those years, all the way up to his death in 1642, Galileo repeatedly claimed that he was the first to use the telescope, the first to observe the moons of Jupiter, and the first to observe the "New Star" in 1604. In his collected works, *Opere*, Galileo goes so far as to say that it was he,

---

[29] See "The Invention of the Telescope," by Albert Van Helden, *Transactions of the American Philosophical Society*, Vol. 67, No. 4; and "Galileo's First Telescopes at Padua and Venice," by Stillman Drake, *Isis*, Vol. 50, No. 3

and he alone, who was the sole inventor of the telescope. None of these claims are true.

Experiments on magnification, using the concave/convex lens method employed by Galileo, had been going on for several centuries before Galileo, including in the manufacture of eyeglasses, "spyglasses," and other simple devices. Almost 100 years before Galileo, Leonardo da Vinci had designed a telescope of the convex/concave lens type, as described in the *Codex Atlanticus*. All of this was so well known at the time, that in the years following 1609, many Italian scholars, including Girolamo Fracastoro and Giovanibaptista Della Porta denounced Galileo's telescope as "not an invention," claiming that the use of optical "glasses," utilizing convex and concave lenses was already widely known.

Galileo presents his telescope to the Doge of Venice

As to the actual "Galileo telescope" itself, the evidence is overwhelming and conclusive that that specific device was not invented by Galileo at all, but rather was invented in the

Netherlands in the autumn of 1608. Three Dutchmen claimed authorship: Hans Lipperhay applied for a patent on a telescope to the States General on Oct. 2, 1608; Jacob Metius likewise applied for a patent of a similar instrument on Oct. 15, 1608; Sacharias Janssen never applied for a patent, but he claimed to have invented the telescope before either Lipperhay or Metius, and years later, writing in his private journal, the Dutch mathematician Isaac Beeckman reports that Janssen's son had told him that his father had built a telescope in 1604, based on the concave/convex lens model.

Whoever was first among the three Dutch inventors, it is clear that all three individuals were in possession of a "Galileo-type" telescope by Nov. 1, 1608, long before Galileo had even heard of it. Additionally, the Englishman Thomas Digges carried out astronomical observations in the late 16th century, employing the use of a "spyglass," very similar to the later Dutch instruments, and in the autumn of 1608, the astronomer Simon Marius built a telescope, based on reports he had received of the Dutch model.

To fully comprehend the massive fraud that was perpetrated in the promotion of Galileo's telescope "discoveries," consider the following chronology:

- October, 1608 - Lipperhay and Metius both apply for telescope patents to the Dutch States General.
- November, 1608 - Paolo Sarpi becomes the *first person in Italy* to hear the news about the "Dutch" telescope, in a letter he receives from Francesco Castrino, writing from the Netherlands.
- January, 1609 - Sarpi writes to Jerome Groslot in Paris, informing him of the Dutch discovery.
- April, 1609 - reports circulate that copies of the Dutch telescope have appeared in Paris

- June, 1609 - Sarpi first informs Galileo about the Dutch telescope and asks Galileo to build one. *This is the first that Galileo had heard of the telescope.*
- July, 1609 - A "foreigner" (whose identity is now lost) arrives in Venice and offers to sell a copy of the Dutch telescope to the Venetian Senate. Sarpi examines the telescope, gets the Venetian government to expel the "foreigner," and then passes on the information, including the construction and components of the telescope, to Galileo.
- July 26, 1609 - Sarpi receives a letter from Jacques Badovere in Paris, informing him that copies of the Dutch telescope are in use throughout Paris.
- Mid-August, 1609 - Galileo informs Sarpi, that after two months of work, he has succeeded in building a telescope.
- Aug. 21, 1609 - first demonstration of Galileo's telescope, from the top of the tower of St. Mark in Venice (arranged by Sarpi)
- Aug. 24, 1609 - demonstration of the telescope to the Doge and the entire Venetian Senate (also arranged by Sarpi)
- 1611 - A Polish visitor to Venice, by the name of Rey, writes in a letter, that the "advisor, author, and director" of the Venetian telescope project had been Paolo Sarpi.

Actually, Galileo appears to have had a lot of trouble building the telescope. During July and August of 1609, Sarpi sent a number of inquiries to Galileo, asking him what was taking so long, particularly given the fact that, for all practical purposes, he had been given rudimentary blueprints for the device. On top of this, Galileo actually had a huge advantage, in that the Italian glass-making industry, which supplied the material for his lenses, was the most advanced in Europe.

Unlike the fraudulent Galileo, an actual *invention* came from Kepler himself. Upon receiving a model of the "Galileo telescope" in early 1610, Kepler immediately realized a fundamental design flaw, and proceeded to actually invent his own original telescope, known as the Kepler or "Astronomical" telescope, utilizing – for the first time – 2 convex lenses, rather than the Dutch model of a concave lens and a convex lens. In 1611 Kepler published *Dioptrice*, an in depth study of lenses and images, in which he described his new invention. Kepler's telescope was far superior and eventually replaced the Galileo telescope in use throughout Europe.

Marketing the Galileo Commodity

Before proceeding to how the myth of Galileo was promulgated throughout Europe, it is first essential – if shocking to some – to grasp the reality that Galileo Galilei was not a scientist. He was a *commodity*, one whom Sarpi invented and then marketed, in a manner that would have made the slickest 1960's New York ad-man green with envy. This was truly one of the most outrageous con-jobs in all of history.

In 1592 Galileo moved to Padua from Pisa, where he had been an undistinguished professor and mathematician. Upon his arrival in Padua he was taken under the wing of a powerful group of Venetian aristocrats, led by Giovanni Francesco Sagredo and Nicolo Contarini. Members of Paolo Sarpi's inner circle, these individuals introduced Galileo into the *Morosini* and *Nave d'Oro ridotti*. The wealthy Sagredo became the personal patron of the young Pisan professor, inviting him to stay at his palatial villa, built on top of Roman ruins on the banks of the Brenta canal. This villa, which was notorious in its day as the scene of wild parties, became Galileo's second home.

Sarpi deployed members of his clique to control and guide Galileo's work, and in some cases provide him with inventions or theories which would then be publicized under Galileo's name. These latter included the first modern thermometer (Sagredo's invention); Galileo's "theory of tides" (developed by de Dominis, and given to Galileo, it was egregiously wrong anyway); and much of his reputed work on mechanics and weights (provided by Santorio Santorio and Filippo Salviati). The idea was to build up the image of Galileo as the hero of the "New Science."

When Sarpi's agents were unable to provide Galileo with new discoveries which he could claim as his own, they simply stole them from others, frequently attacking the original discoverer as a plagiarist (a method to be employed a century later against Leibniz's authorship of the calculus). The event which is often pointed to as the opening salvo of Galileo's assault on Aristotelianism, was his 1604 announcement that he had discovered a "New Star" (actually a super-nova). The only problem is that the New Star was discovered weeks earlier by the astronomer Simon Marius.[30] Upon making the discovery, Marius had dispatched his student Baldassare Capra to Padua. Capra passed the news of the discovery to Paolo Sarpi, who then personally gave it to Galileo, who subsequently proclaimed the discovery to be his own.

Later, in 1607, this same Baldassare Capra became involved in another fight with Galileo, when Capra claimed the invention of the Geometer's Compass in his work *Usus*

---

[30] "Was Simon Mayr Galileo's 'Ancient Adversary' in 1607?", by Stillman Drake, *Isis*, Vol. 67, No. 3.

et Fabrica Circini. Galileo accused Capra of plagiarism, and on orders from the Giovani-controlled Venetian Senate, all 450 copies of Capra's book were seized and burned. During this controversy, it was Sarpi who personally mediated the dispute on behalf of the Venetian government, and judged in favor of Galileo.

Simon Marius had a second, more serious run-in with Galileo in 1610, when Marius became the first astronomer in Europe to observe the moons of Jupiter. When Galileo proclaimed the discovery as his own, Marius publicly attacked him. The Sarpi group launched a massive campaign against Marius accusing him of plagiarism, and for the next three centuries historians dutifully gave credit to Galileo for the discovery. However, in 1900, an international scientific conference re-examined the Galileo/Marius dispute. They determined that Marius had been falsely accused, and concluded that he was the true discoverer of Jupiter's moons.

The same plagiarism gambit was used yet again in 1612, when the Bavarian astronomer Christopher Scheiner reported that he had seen spots on the sun, using a telescope of Kepler's design. Almost immediately Galileo announced that he had been observing sun-spots for over a year, and so had priority of discovery, a surprising claim, since Galileo had never previously mentioned sun-spots.

To the extent Galileo actually had a "scientific method" at all, it was taken entirely from Sarpi, as can be seen in Galileo's fawning praise, "No one in Europe, it can be said without exaggeration, surpasses Master Paolo Sarpi in the knowledge of the science of mathematics." In addition, it is clear that a key to the Venetian control of Galileo was through the purse string. His original move from Pisa to Padua was motivated by a tripling of his salary. Later he was the beneficiary of Sagredo's "favors," and in 1623, after

Galileo had left Venice, and was in difficult circumstances, Sarpi personally arranged for him to receive a Venetian pension, i.e., a permanent monetary stipend, keeping him on a lifelong financial string. In the 1630s Sarpi's secretary, Fulgenzio Micanzio paid extra money to Galileo for the writing of both *The Dialogue Concerning Two Chief World Systems* and *The Discourses on Two New Sciences*. The 1638 *Discourses* was then smuggled out of Italy by Micanzio, who arranged for it to be published in Leyden. By then the marketing of Galileo was in full swing, and salons promoting the new science of empiricism were flourishing in Paris, Rome, the Netherlands, and other locations.

Galileo's real epitaph can be best expressed in his own words: "What has philosophy got to do with measuring anything?"

The Mersenne Circle

Following the publication of *Sidereus Nuncius* in 1610, there was a proliferation of "scientific" groups throughout Europe, all aimed at promoting the new science of empiricism, and all taking their cue from the developments in Venice. Among the most important of these groups were the *Academia dei Lincei* in Rome, the Oxford Philosophical Club (a.k.a. the Invisible College) – the forerunner of the British Royal Society – in England, and the *Academia Parisiensis*, – the so-called Mersenne Circle – based in Paris.

The Mersenne Circle came into existence in 1623, and lasted for about 25 years, when, after the death of Mersenne, Pierre Gassendi organized a successor group, the *Acadamie Montmor*, which lasted about another 20 years. The Mersenne Circle was unquestionably the most important group in Europe in promoting Galileo and spreading the new science of empiricism. It was also at the

Mersenne Circle that the direct transition was made from Galileo to Descartes.

The founder of the Circle, the ordained priest Marin Mersenne, began as a staunch defender of Aristotelean scholasticism, and had gone so far as to issue a public attack on Galileo in the early 1620s. By the 1630s, however, Mersenne had surrendered to empiricism. He became Galileo's foremost champion in all northern Europe, and it was Mersenne who was responsible for the translation and publication of Galileo's works in France. Mersenne is perhaps best known today for his 1636 work *L'harmonie Universelle*, an attempt to apply Sarpi's empirical methods to music.[31] Mersenne was also the key Parisian contact of Rene Descartes. He met Descartes in 1623, and by no later than 1630 he was Descartes' chief partisan in Paris. When Descartes finished his *Meditations*, the first person he sent it to was Mersenne, who circulated it in transcript form, showing it to Hobbes and other members of the Circle.

At the beginning the Circle was not a homogeneous group. The key leaders, Mersenne, Pierre Gassendi, Isaac Beeckman, Fabri Peiresc, and Thomas Hobbes were all in the empiricist camp. However, other individuals like Blaise Pascal, Pierre Fermat, and Christian Huygens were also sometimes participants. As was the case of Galileo's

---

[31] In addition to Mersenne, one of the leaders of the empiricist attacks on music was Galileo's father, Vincenzo Galilei. Together with his associates in the Florentine *Camerata*, Galilei carried out extensive "experimental" work on acoustics, vibrating strings, and columns of air, and promoted his own version of "equal-temperament." Others involved in this attack on Renaissance music included Rene Descartes, who published, with the aid of Isaac Beeckman, *Compendium Musicae*, and the Venetian G.B. Benedetti, In his *Harmony of the World*, Kepler attacked this empiricist approach to music, calling Galilei's mathematical approach "clever tempering," but adding, "for theorizing and even more for investigating the nature of melody, I consider it ruinous." (Book 3, Chapter 8)

contacts with Kepler, one of the purposes of the Circle was to recruit, co-opt, or neutralize the opponents of empiricism. The activity of the Circle centered on a sustained, relentless attack on established Aristotelianism. Rene Descartes participated in the Circle by no later than 1625, and the Circle was crucial in spreading Descartes' influence. The political exile Hugo Grotius also attended meetings.

Other than Mersenne, the two key leaders of the Circle were Gassendi and Beeckman. A professor of mathematics at the *College Royal*, Gassendi publicly broke with Aristotelianism in 1624 with the publication of his *Exercitationes Paradoxicae*. An extreme materialist, Gassendi stated that all we know is from the senses, that our access to knowledge is

Marin Mersenne

limited to the appearance of what we know, and that universals are fictions. He is known for his "atomist matter theory," and he agreed with Descartes that space and time are uniformly and infinitely extended.

Gassendi's closest friend was Nicolas-Claude Fabri de Peiresc. Peiresc studied for three years at Padua University, knew both Sarpi and Galileo personally, and became a public supporter of Galileo after the publication of *Sidereus Nuncius* in 1610. Gassendi was also very close to Thomas Hobbes, and by the mid-1600s many of Gassendi's works were translated and published in England, where they were studied by Locke, Boyle, and Newton.

Pierre Gassendi

The 17th century spread of empiricism was not an academic "natural phenomenon." After 1610 it was a centrally deployed campaign, directed from Venice. The key colony was the Paris-Netherlands axis defined by the Mersenne-Gassendi network, with a second group in England centered around Francis Bacon. The Paris group was the center of support for Galileo, and its influence radiated throughout the continent. It was also the launching pad for Descartes. The coordination of the Venice-Paris-Netherlands triangle was tight. Leading members of the circle communicated directly with Micanzio, and Galileo in Italy (earlier, some had been in touch with Sarpi before his death in 1623). Beeckman and Descartes were in continual communication with Mersenne, and traveled to Paris for personal consultation; similarly, Mersenne, Gassendi, and other Parisians made regular pilgrimages to the Netherlands.

At the time of Galileo's trial before the inquisition in 1633, it was the Mersenne Circle that rushed to his defense. Gassendi wrote letters of support for Galileo to use in his defense at the trial, and, after the guilty verdict, members of the Circle organized an attempt to bring Galileo out of Italy and obtain political asylum for him in the Netherlands. The leader of this effort was Hugo Grotius, with Mersenne acting as the go-between with Galileo. Their agent in the

Netherlands was Martinus Hortensius, an Amsterdam professor who had played a key role in circulating Galileo's works in the Netherlands. Hortensius also published an attack on Kepler, saying that astronomy should be based on observation and mathematical demonstration, not on speculation. He corresponded with both Galileo and Descartes, and in reward for faithful efforts, in 1637, Galileo sent him his original 1610 telescope.

Eventually, Galileo made the decision to stay in Italy. Some say the reason was failing health, others claim it was from fear of the Inquisition. Perhaps he just didn't want to give up his regular paychecks from Micanzio. Whatever the reason, he remained under arrest, and his "martyrdom" was used to weave the web of empiricism across Europe.

Descartes

The Frenchman Rene Descartes lived most of his adult life in the Netherlands, and it was there he was recruited by the mathematician Isaac Beeckman. Beeckman's influence on Descartes must have been profound; Descartes describes him as his teacher in mathematics and mechanics, and it was Beeckman who introduced him to Mersenne, the association which "made" Descartes as a major scientific figure. During all of his years in the Netherlands, Descartes was under the protection of the House of Orange, but it was not until after his death in 1650, particularly during the "True Freedom" period of the DeWitt brothers, that Descartes' Cartesianism became truly hegemonic in the Netherlands.

Descartes' mathematical work was a continuation of the empiricist methods of Sarpi and Galileo. Descartes' universe was one of linear extension into an infinitely extended void, a universe without singularities, and without human creativity.

In 1632, the *Athenaeum,* an Amsterdam school for the sons of the new Dutch elite, was established, and it was there that Cartesianism made its first inroads into Dutch academic life. Later, in 1694, supporters of Descartes at the *Athenaeum* published the first complete edition of his works.

From the *Athenaeum,* the Descartes' influence spread to the universities. The first university to officially teach Descartes' philosophy was the University of Utrecht, in 1635. In 1653 a Cartesian study group was established at the University of Leyden, based on the idea that all physical processes can be defined in mathematical terms. At Leyden, Cartesianism quickly dominated the medical and biological faculty.

In 1659 Johann DeWitt, the leader of Holland, translated and published Descartes' *La Geometric,* with an original appendix written by himself.

By the 1670s the Cartesians were hegemonic at all the Dutch universities.[32]

The Cavendish Family & England

In examining the subversion of England by the agents of Paolo Sarpi – including Hobbes, Bacon, Wotton, and Petty – it is shocking, at first, to find the name Cavendish pop up again and again and again. What complicates matters even further, is that there are not one or two, but FIVE William Cavendishes who were involved in the Venetian takeover of England. This role of the Cavendish clan begins with Sarpi himself and continues all the way into the 18th century. Every step of the way, they were to play an important role

---

[32] *The Calvinist Copernicans: The Reception of the New Astronomy in the Dutch Republic,* by Rienk Vermij, Amsterdam: Edita KNAW

in the creation of the Anglo-Dutch Empire.

To sort some of this out, I present here brief profiles of the Five Williams, in chronological order:

1. **William Cavendish, First Earl of Devonshire** (1552-1626) - the individual who financially backed Thomas Hobbes from 1610 to 1626, and employed Hobbes in 1610 to tutor his son.

2. **William Cavendish, Second Earl of Devonshire** (1590-1628) - the William who, in 1614, accompanied Hobbes on a trip to Venice where they both met with Paolo Sarpi. Following this trip, Cavendish maintained a 13 year correspondence with Sarpi and Micanzio. This was the Cavendish who initiated the correspondence between Sarpi and Francis Bacon in 1616. He was also a founding Director of the Virginia Company, and remained close to Hobbes his entire life.

3. **William Cavendish, First Duke of Newcastle** (1592-1676) - nephew of the First Earl of Devonshire and first cousin of the Second Earl. In 1611 he traveled with Henry Wotton – Sarpi's supporter during the Interdict crisis – to Savoy, when Wotton was named the new English ambassador there. This William organized the informal "Welbeck Academy" at his estate in England, which became the center for Galileo supporters in England, with members translating many of Galileo's works into English, including the *Dialogue Concerning the Two Chief World Systems*, in 1636. Newcastle and other members of his Academy, then played an important role in organizing the Mersenne Circle in Paris, and

Newcastle, himself, became an early patron of Mersenne.[33] In 1634 Newcastle sent Hobbes to Paris to work with Mersenne. Later, Newcastle spent three years in Paris, from 1645 to 1648 , where he played an important role in supporting the activities of the Mersenne group, including personal financial sponsorship of Hobbes, Gassendi, and Descartes. Late in life he became a patron and financial backer of William Petty.

4. **William Cavendish, Third Earl of Devonshire** (1617-1684) - son of the Second Earl of Devonshire, this William also became a pupil of Hobbes for 7 years in Paris, from 1631-1638, during Hobbes' time with the Mersenne Circle. In 1635 Hobbes and Devonshire traveled to Italy and met with Galileo.

5. **William Cavendish, First Duke of Devonshire** (1640-1707) - son of the Third Earl of Devonshire. A Whig leader, he was one of the "Immortal Seven" who signed the Invitation to William in 1688, asking the Dutch William of Orange to invade England. This William was also Abraham De Moivre's first political sponsor in England. A member of the Royal Society, it was William who first gave De Moivre a copy of Newton's *Principia Mathematica*. Both William's son

---

[33] *Thomas Hobbes and the Duke of Newcastle: A Study in the Mutuality of Patronage before the Establishment of the Royal Society,* by Lisa T. Sarasohn

James, and his nephew Charles (also both later members of the Royal Society) were pupils of De Moivre.

One thing that is clear from looking at this snapshot of the "5 Williams," is that Thomas Hobbes was a virtual *Golem* of the Cavendish family. He was protected and financed by the Devonshire branch from 1610-1628, then again from 1631 to 1638, and then picked up by the Newcastle branch in the 1640s (this is the period when he wrote both *The Leviathan* and *De Cive*). In 1679 Hobbes died while residing at the Cavendish family estate in England.

By no later than 1621, the key nexus of the Venetian faction in England was the Sarpi (and later Micanzio)-Cavendish-Bacon-Hobbes network, and it is clear that this was a breathing, living network, whose activities were closely coordinated. Sarpi was corresponding with both Cavendish and Bacon. Hobbes was serving as the personal secretary to Bacon, and translating his works into Latin, while Micanzio was translating them into Italian and publishing them in Venice. Bacon's influence grew in the years following his death, leading into the founding of the Oxford Group, and ultimately the Royal Society by his disciples.

The end product of all this was, of course, Isaac Newton, who began by studying Gassendi, moved on to Descartes, and ultimately arrived at Bacon—a true end product of a Sarpi curriculum. And when the publication of Newton's works, including his *Principia Mathematica*, failed to have the intended impact, it was Venice once again that stepped in to help. The 1715-1718 visit of Venetian master-spy Antonio Conti to England resulted in the "creation" of Newton as the master scientist, just as Sarpi had "created" Galileo a hundred years earlier. Conti's subsequent deployment of Newton against Leibniz shouldn't have shocked anyone. It was just Sarpi using Galileo against Kepler, all over again.

VI. The Legal Theorists of the Oligarchical Model

Francisco de Vitoria

The Anglo-Dutch Liberal doctrine of money, is merely a deluded belief induced in the believer, to the intended advantage of the system which crafts and spreads that delusion on behalf of its own, intended, predatory advantage.

Lyndon H. LaRouche Jr. - *The New Politics*

Beginning with the creation of the Spanish and Portuguese empires, and proceeding into the emergence of the Dutch and British empires, new legal doctrines were required to justify these modern oligarchic entities. During this evolutionary stage of transforming the Empire, there was never at any time an abandonment of the ancient Roman/feudal view that the vast majority of mankind were virtually sub-human, with no innate rights, deserving to be exploited and enslaved. However, with the emergence of the trans-oceanic empires alongside the Venetian-modeled financial centers of Amsterdam and London, new theories were required to determine how this new version of Empire would be governed. This chapter will examine some of those theories.

The Spanish Origins of Free Trade

In 1526, 34 years after Columbus' first trans-Atlantic voyage, the Spanish Dominican scholar Francisco de Vitoria was appointed the Chair of Theology at the University of Salamanca in Spain. For the next 20 years, Vitoria recruited a group of followers, who produced a vast body of work encompassing theology, economics, natural law and jurisprudence. Taken together, these individuals and their writings became known as the School of Salamanca. The epistemological influence of the Salamancans was pervasive, even into the 18th century. Ironically, the greatest impact of their collective work was in the Protestant north, particularly in the cities of Amsterdam and London. Recently, interest in the Salamanca School has been revived, primarily through the efforts of the Von Mises Institute, and other free-trade fanatics of the Austrian school of economics. The only modern work on the school, Marjorie Grice-Hutchinson's *School of Salamanca*, actually contains a dedication to Friedrich Hayek.

Many of the more mature theories of free trade and monetarism, which emerged later in the writings of Grotius, John Locke, and others, had their origins in the theories of the Salamanca School. Therefore, an examination of their work is essential at this point. To flesh this out, immediately below are profiles of Vitoria and his most important disciples:

Francisco de Vitoria - reportedly, the closest advisor to the Hapsburg Emperor Charles V, and subsequently a confidant of his son, King Philip II, Vitoria founded his school at a time of rapid expansion of the Spanish Empire. This empire was largely financed through banks in Augsburg, Antwerp, and Genoa, all of which were dominated by Venetian interests. Vitoria, and his students at Salamanca, became the empire's propagandists and theorists, and they crafted economic policies as well as what one might call a "Code of Ultramontane International Law," intended to justify the new colonialism.

Between 1527 and 1540, Vitoria delivered a series of lectures which were transcribed into several works, including *De Indis et de Ivre Belli Relectiones* and *De Juri Belli Hispanorum in Barbaros*, and subsequently published in Lyons, Salamanca, Antwerp, and Venice. Although his pupils would develop more sophisticated concepts of monetary value, the germ of the Salamancan free market ideology is all in Vitoria. The two main issues which de Vitoria, himself, focuses on are "property rights" and "just war."

A major influence on Vitoria was Alfonso Tostado, the Bishop of Avila, whose collected works were later published in Giovani-controlled Venice in 1596. Tostado wrote extensively on the subject of "just war," and said:

> "In a just war everything that a man can seize becomes the property of its captor, both by divine law and the Law of Nations; and it is just to kill... in a just war there is nothing that may not be wrought upon the enemy... Wars are just when they are undertaken in order to redress for injuries, restitution of property, or recompense for wrongs done."

Taking Tostado's anti-human ravings as his starting point, Vitoria proceeded to create an entire theory of international law which justified the exploitation and enslavement of native populations. In doing so, he explicitly rejected the Medieval argument that it is allowable to enslave non-Christian populations for theological reasons, i.e., because they are non-Christian. Instead, Vitoria, using many passages from Roman Law, developed an argument defending slavery based on "property rights." Vitoria stated that religion is not a legitimate justification for war; that the only cause for a "just war" is injury suffered in violation of the Law of Nations. He asks, "what may be done in a Just War?" His answer, "everything that is necessary to recover lost property, and its value."

Vitoria's argument begins by stating that the Indians of the Western Hemisphere actually have legitimate self-governing societies. Despite their backwardness, and idolatry, they possess true *dominium*. Neither the right of discovery (*inventio*), nor the right for religious missionary work justify conquest. Vitoria says, "According to the Law of Nations (i.e. Roman Law), that which has no owner becomes the property of the seizer; but the possessions we are speaking of (i.e. the land and possessions of the Indians) were under a master, and therefore they do not come under the head of discovery."

Vitoria's catch, however, is that because the Indians possess true *dominium*, they are bound to the strictures of the Law of Nations (*jus gentium*). This means they must abide by certain universally recognized freedoms, including freedom of trade and open borders. The Law of Nations requires the Indians to allow Spain free and open commerce. The Indians are also obliged to share with Spain any property they hold in common. If the Indians infringe on these rights, the Spanish are permitted to wage total "just war" upon them, including seizing their land and possessions, delivering them into slavery, and exacting reparations.

In *De Indis*, Vitoria says "neither may the native princes hinder their subjects from carrying on trade with the Spanish, nor, on the other hand, may the princes of Spain prevent commerce with the natives." Vitoria rejects the idea of absolute sovereignty of nations, and asserts the right of free trade as superior to governments or nation-states. Vitoria's argument is a complete theory of free trade and the supremacy of the *fondi*.

Domingo de Soto - an early Salamancan who studied directly under Vitoria, later succeeding him as first theology Chair at Salamanca University, De Soto headed the Spanish delegation to the Council of Trent. De Soto was one of the first to insist that usury is compatible with the medieval idea of "just price." In his ten volume treatise *De Justitia et Jure*, he says, "The rule 'a thing is worth whatever it can be sold for,' is a celebrated axiom among jurisconsults. Therefore,... we should leave merchants to fix the price of their wares;" and, "A man may do as he likes with his own property." He also bitterly opposed all efforts for relief of the poor.

Fernando Vasquez de Menchaca – In reading de Menchaca, one is struck that John Locke must have owned a copy of his works, since Locke repeats many of de Menchaca arguments, almost verbatim, in his *Two Treatises of Government*. De Menchaca argues that private life and private interests predate and have precedence over the state.   Private property is an institution of the *jus gentium*; it is not a creature of the *jus civile* (civil law). The state exists solely to protect the institution of private property.   The state, therefore, has limited power (i.e., limited sovereignty):   it has the right of *dominium jurisdictiones* (a limited jurisdiction to punish crime), but not *dominium proprietatis* (the right of ownership).   A citizen's private ownership is inviolable. The *jus gentium* postulates a universal "private sector" human community (what some today call a "shareholder" society). Perversely, Vasquez justifies his views with the assertion that they all flow from the concept that man is made in the image of God! Man possesses *dominium* in his nature. The command to pursue *dominium*, made in *Genesis I*, was a command to take possession of parts of nature. By doing this man expresses his freedom, and acts in the image of God. His private property is essential to human culture. Society's power is based on the human individual, property rights, the family, and the right of free communication/exchange.

Martin de Azpilcueta Navarro (Navarrus) – perhaps the most influential of the Salamanca economic theorists,[34] (with the possible exception of Lessius), Navarrus also had the distinction of being the only major Salamancan to have a personal friendship with Paolo Sarpi. When Sarpi was in Rome in 1586, and was having a very difficult time (he was under attack from the Roman Curia), he was befriended by the 93 year old Navarrus, who provided him much-needed political protection.

Navarrus' main work on monetary theory, the *Comentarios de Usura*, presents the first thorough examination of foreign exchanges ever written. Navarrus practically created the Salamancan "Quantity Theory of Money,"[35] which, among other things, rabidly opposed government interference in the free marketplace, including

Martin de Azpilcueta Navarro

---

[34] "Scholastic Morality and the Birth of Economics: the Thought of Martin de Azpilcueta," by Rodrio Munoz de Juana, *Journal of Markets and Morality*, Vol. 4. No 1

[35] John Law's *Money and Trade Considered*, published in 1705, contains a theory of value identical to the Salamancans

actions like price controls. Among the Salamancans, Navarrus is also the most forceful in his rejection of the economic views of Aristotle and Thomas Aquinas. Navarrus explicitly defends money-changing and usury, stating that for a nation's currency to settle at its correct value, it is essential that it be openly traded at a profit. He says, "Nor is it true that to use money by changing it at a profit is against nature. Although that is not the first and principal use for which money was invented, it is none the less an important secondary use." Even more extraordinary, the development of financial derivatives is also defended by Navarrus. He argues in favor of the legitimacy of futures contracts, and, again, attacks Aristotle on the issue of financial speculation. Navarro writes, "Aristotle thought it wrong, this art of exchanging and dealing in the exchange of monies. We say that if it is exercised as it ought to be, then it is licit. Nor is it true that the use of money, exchanging it in order to make more money, goes against nature."

Diego de Covarrubias y Leiva – a pupil of Navarrus, Covarrubias was one of the great experts on Roman Law, sometimes called the "Spanish Bartolus." He categorically rejected the idea of absolute state sovereignty. He also developed a "subjective theory of value." In 1550 he published *Veterum numismatum collatio*, on the quantity theory of money. He said "the value of an article does not depend on its essential nature but on the estimation of men, even if that estimation is foolish." He said that the just price of an item does not depend on its original cost, nor on the cost of labor or production, but only on the market-value.

Leonard de Leys (Lessius) – a native of Belgium, in the Spanish Netherlands, Lessius spent years studying the

Antwerp financial markets. His writings were highly influential. His major work, *De justitia et jure* went through 40 editions in Antwerp, Paris, Lyons, and Venice.[36] Lessius wrote extensively on the nature of what he calls the "fortuitous" value of money. He states that this fortuitous value is based on four things: the abundance or scarcity of money, the demand that exists for bills of exchange, the supply of bills of exchange, the demand for money. Lessius also wrote on the subject of risk, as it relates to insurance contracts, and the role of interest rates in financial transactions.

Francisco Suarez - Suarez writings on International Law influenced John Locke, Hugo Grotius, Alberico Gentili, Johannes Althusius and Samuel Puffendorf. Grotius called Suarez the "greatest and most precise of the philosophers and theologians," and Suarez's pluralist free-market views on international law are incorporated, almost in toto, in Grotius' works, particularly in *De Jure Praedae*. In his two major works, *Tractatus de Legibus* and *Defensor Fidei*, Suarez presents an uncompromising view of limited national sovereignty. He states that the sovereignty of the individual state is limited by the fact that it forms part of a community of nations, linked by mutual obligations. His writings focus on the issue of international law, and he develops a distinction between the Law of Nations and a pluralistic view of local customary law, which is rooted in instinct. Suarez says that within cultures the great motivators are passions and desires, and that international agreements are necessary to keep those baser passions in restraint.

As stated above, the influence of the Salamancans was

---

[36] "The Legal and Scholastic Roots of Leonardus Lessius Economic Thought," by Louis Baeck, *Journal of Economic Thought*, #37

pervasive. Much of what is in John Law, François Quesnay, and Adam Smith can be found in their writings on economic theory. Their ideas were still influencing the currency policies of the British oligarchy into the 19th century. They were also the *first* group to write systematically on the subject of currency exchange transactions, and the *first* to put forward a developed notion of the so-called "subjective" theory of value, in regards to both currencies and other commodities.

More important was their immediate impact on the development of the new financial center in Amsterdam. The 17th century transformation of Amsterdam into the banking capital of the world would not have been possible without the prior innovations at the Antwerp Bourse, and it was in the Antwerp of the Spanish Netherlands, that the theories of the Salamancans had their most profound impact. Three of the crucial elements which made the "success" of the Antwerp Bourse possible were, a relaxation of legal constraints on financial activity, a wildly reductionist view of the nature of money, and the emergence of a radical concept of "property rights," all of which were pioneered by the Salamancans.

The Calvinists: Pluralism vs. the Commonwealth

"Sic semper tyrannis" - John Wilkes Booth, April 14, 1865

Beginning in the 1570s a series of books were published, mostly by Calvinist Huguenot authors, which have come to be associated with the term, the "Right of Resistance." Politically, many of these authors were tied to political or religious organizations that served as the "cats-paws" for Venice in her design to provoke religious war between the reactionary Hapsburg-Vatican alliance and the Protestants. But their real importance lies elsewhere. Under the guise of opposing the tyranny of the Catholic Party, and in the wake of the St. Bartholomew's Day massacre of thousands of French Protestants, these authors formulated new theories of government and society, which represented an actual subversion of Cusa's Renaissance idea of the *Commonwealth,* redefining the term to fit a new imperial vision of a society based on the law of the marketplace and oligarchical property rights.[37]   In the process they also contributed to the emergence of impotent parliamentary methods of government.

Between 1573 and 1579, four books were issued which elaborated the Calvinists' new theories. These were Francois Hotman's *Francogallia,* Theodore Beza's *De jure magistratuum,* the anonymous *Vindiciae contra tyrannos,* and George Buchanan's *De Jure Regni apud Scotos.* Others associated with this network include Dennis Godefroy and Hubert Languet.   Cumulatively, these authors were denounced as "monarchomachs" (king killers) by their enemies, because one theme that was common to all of them is that societies have a natural law right to resist monarchical tyranny, even by means of regicide.

Several of them, like Languet and Hotman were personal friends of Paolo Sarpi. Buchanan had been educated by the Salamancans in Portugal. Beza was the successor to Jean Calvin as the head of the Geneva Church. Almost all of them had backgrounds as university professors in Roman Law.

The most famous and influential of these Calvinist works was the *Vindiciae Contra Tyrannos* ("A Defense of Liberty Against Tyrants"). Its author is unknown, but most experts,

---

[37] The premier example of this fraudulent sophistry is Oliver Cromwell's so-called "Commonwealth"

both at the time and since, ascribe it to Paolo Sarpi's close ally Phillipe du Plessis-Mornay. The *Vindiciae* is usually described as a defense against monarchical tyranny, and, in reading it today, parts of it seem very reasonable. However, it is the way Mornay twists those apparently reasonable arguments, which makes the work truly Delphic.

There are four parts to the *Vindiciae*, and the first two, which deal with the right to resist religious oppression, are very straightforward. Mornay says, "God must rather be obeyed than men." Fair enough. But it is the third part which is the key, for here Mornay raises the issue of non-religious oppression, and asks, "whether it be lawful to resist a prince who doth oppress or ruin a public state." How does one define non-religious oppression, and how grievous must that oppression be to justify revolt? To answer that, I will give some quotes, and it is important to follow the direction in which Mornay takes the argument to get the full impact of what he is actually saying:

> "The people establish kings, and put the sceptre into their hands... Now, seeing that the people choose and establish their kings, it follows that the whole body of the people is above the king."

So far, so good. . . but then,

> "It being then so that every one loves that which is his own, in the creation of kings, men gave not their own proper goods unto them... A king may challenge and gain right to the kingdom of Germany, France and England, and yet, notwithstanding, he may not lawfully take any honest man's estate from him."

Mornay then takes this argument further and states that the only non-religious justification for resistance against a monarch is if the monarch threatens the life or the property of the populace. Mornay bases this argument on a concept he calls "popular sovereignty," i.e., that God's covenant is with the people, not with a Monarch or the state, and that private property is a fundamental part of that covenant with God. In Mornay's schema, individual property rights, derived from God, pre-date and take precedence over the state. This proposition is actually the direct opposite of both the Commonwealth idea, as well as the principles in the Preamble to the United States Constitution. What Mornay is actually proposing is not a resistance to tyranny, but *resistance to sovereignty.*

However, Mornay goes even further in demonstrating how far removed he is from the idea of "man made in God's image," which is at the heart of the concept of a Commonwealth. He says:

> "The law of nature teaches and commands us to maintain and defend our lives and liberties against all injury and violence. Nature has imprinted this by instinct in dogs against wolves, in bulls against lions, betwixt pigeons and sparrow-hawks, betwixt pullen and kites, and yet much more in man against man himself, if man become a beast: and therefore he who questions the lawfulness of defending oneself, does, as much as in him lies, question the law of nature."

This is Roman Law's bestial view of man in its most naked form.

Although the influence of Mornay and the other "Right to Resistance" authors was centered in Geneva, the Netherlands, among the French Huguenots, and other Calvinist areas, their books were widely circulated and impacted all of Protestant Europe. Much of what exists in

John Locke's "Social Contract" theory, can be found in the writings of Mornay and his associates.

Hugo Grotius justifies the new Empire

Even today, when many of his ideas are considered outmoded, Hugo Grotius exerts a lasting influence on international law, the "law of the seas," and corporate law. Grotius, himself was not a particularly original thinker. His work incorporates the ideas of many others, including Alberico Gentili, Francois Hotman, and the Salamancans Vitoria, Suarez, and Covarruvias. He praises Suarez to the skies, and he specifically cites Vitoria as the source for his views on "Just War." More than anything, Grotius writings are a synthesis of these other earlier and contemporary works.

The key thing about Grotius is that he was a high-ranking official of the Dutch East India Company, the *Vereenigde Oostindische Compagnie* (VOC). Founded in 1602 by Grotius' political ally Johan van Oldenbarneveldt, the VOC was both the paradigm for the new maritime Empire corporation, as well as one of the three pillars of the new financial monolith in Amsterdam. With the creation of this Amsterdam-based empire, the triumph of the Venetian system over the Renaissance idea of the Commonwealth was realized. The VOC employee Grotius was explicit in his view that private property rights and the conduct of the markets could not be constrained by the power of government. A clearer example of this can not be found then this 1644 policy statement by the Board of Directors of the VOC:

"The places and strongholds which the VOC has captured in the East Indies should not be regarded as national conquests, but as the property of private merchants, who were entitled to sell these places to whomsoever they wished, even if it was the King of Spain."

Anticipating the nature of the British East India Company a century later, the VOC possessed its own independent authority to wage war, to conclude foreign treaties, to build fortresses, and to enlist naval and military personal. Additionally, all employees of the VOC pledged an oath of allegiance to the company. The VOC was not a branch of the Dutch government; theirs was a private empire, which maintained the right to ignore or override the sovereignty of nation states, including their own.

Grotius' two major writings are the *De Jure Praedae Commentaris* (Commentary on the Law of Prize and Booty), and the *De Jure Belli ac Pacis* (The Law of War and Peace). The *De Jure Praedae Commentaris* was written for the directors of the Dutch East India Company, to defend their right to seize Spanish and Portuguese ships and colonies. In justifying the actions of the VOC, Grotius turns again to the writings of the Salamancans. In Chapter 12, he says:

"Freedom of trade, then, springs from the primary law of nations, which has a natural and permanent cause, so that it cannot be abrogated... I shall base my argument on the following most specific and unimpeachable axiom of the Law of Nations (jus gentium), called a primary rule of first principle: Every nation is free to travel to every other nation, and to trade with it...By the law of nations the principle was introduced that the opportunity to engage in trade, of which, no one can be deprived, should be free to all men..."

The *De Jure Belli ac Pacis* is Grotius' premier work on the subject of international law. In it, he spends a good deal of time discussing the valid reasons for waging a "Just War" against another people. He says there are three such reasons: self-defense, defense of property, and serious offenses. Wars over religion are not justified. This argument is, of course, identical to that of Francisco Vitoria. In this work Grotius also says that the law of nations justifies the enslavement of captured enemies.

In another of his works, *The Antiquity of the Ancient Batavians*, Grotius puts forward his notion of a "republic." He says that the best type is an aristocratic republic, and he puts forward two "shining examples" for the political leadership of the Netherlands to emulate: ancient Sparta and Venice. He says:

> "If a foreign parallel of this is required, I find nothing more similar than the Spartan state, which is praised above all others... If we apply reason, it persuades us that power in the state should best be entrusted to the best..., or if we look for parallel cases, the very celebrated examples of Sparta, Carthage, Rhodes..., and as many believe, Rome itself, immediately present themselves... Nor is there a lack of recent examples: Geneva, Genoa and the famous city of Venice, which has proved its stability by its continuity over a thousand years."

Gentili, Althusius, et. al.

At the beginning of the 17th century, with the Giovani in power in Venice, and the Dutch Empire emerging in Amsterdam, other great maritime companies were also founded. The Netherlands may have been in the vanguard, but in London similar initiatives were also underway, including the founding of the Levant Company, the Venice Company, and the (old) East India Company, all between 1586 and 1600. In addition to Grotius and the Salamancans, many others were contributing to the debate on how the new form of Empire should take shape. Two of the most influential of these were Johannes Althusius and Alberico Gentili.

Alberico Gentili lived in the generation immediately prior to Grotius. An Italian Protestant, he fled to England to escape the Inquisition. There he established close friendships with Mornay's friend Philip Sidney and Paolo Sarpi's ally Henry Wooten. Wooten secured for him a position as Oxford University's Regius Professor of Civil Law. At Oxford, his lectures on Roman Law became famous and attracted a devoted following. Gentili's major work was *De Juri Belli Libri Ires*, which is frequently cited by Grotius as a major influence. Like Grotius, Gentili was strongly influenced by both Vitoria and Covarruvias, and he endorses Vitoria's views on "just war" and enslavement of the Indians.

To repeat a point made above, with Grotius (in Amsterdam) and Gentili (in London), you are not dealing simply with theories or philosophy. Their writings were political, and were intended to be both a justification and legal defense for the empires already being created in their own time.

With Johannes Althusius, a Calvinist who lived contemporaneously with Grotius, we find the whole oligarchical witches' brew all in one package. Althusius cites as influences: the Roman *Corpus Juris Civilis*, the "monarchomachs" Francois Hotman, and Phillipe du Plessis Mornay, the Salamancans Francisco Vitoria, Diego

Covarruvias and Francisco Suarez, and the above-mentioned Gentili. For good measure, Althusius attacks Plato as an idealist. Later, Samuel Puffendorf would cite Althusius as the strongest influence on his own work.

Althusius' main work is the *Politics*. Much of what we find later in John Locke is contained in it. He denies the existence of national sovereignty, states that society is composed of a contract among heteronomic individuals, and that property rights are paramount. Additionally, Althusius proposes a fairly detailed scheme of oligarchical government, once again modeled on Sparta. Going so far as to call his proposed ruling class *Ephors* (after Sparta), he says, "Those persons should be elected *ephors* who have great might and wealth, because it is in their interest that the commonwealth be healthy"

John Locke

It is essential to deal with John Locke, even if he really doesn't deserve it. It is clear he is a world-class plagiarizer. Almost all of his economic theories are taken (sometimes almost verbatim) from the Salmancans, his social contract theory is cribbed from Althusius, and even his premier philosophical work, the *Essay Concerning Human Understanding* (of notorious *Tabula Rasa* fame), is nothing more than an elaboration of Paolo Sarpi's *L'Arte di Ben Pensare* (The Art of Thinking Well).[38] There is almost nothing original in any of his works.

Nevertheless, there are two reasons Locke must be dealt with. The first is the minor reason, which is that there is one thing new in Locke – the open face of oligarchical greed

---

[38] See the testimony of the Venetian Doge Marco Foscarini who reports, "What Sarpi says of axioms he says also of first truths and of syllogisms, and this appears to be the source from whence Locke has copied or amplified his ideas..."

and evil, without apologies. In many of the earlier writers whom Locke stole from, there is at least a pretense of religion or justice. Locke doesn't bother. There is no theological veneer; there is no "resistance to tyranny;" there is just money and greed.

However the second, and by far much more important, reason to deal with Locke, is all of the massive lies that have been told, and taught in schools, about his influence on the American Revolution. It was not the American Revolution, but the Glorious Revolution of 1688 which brought William of Orange to the throne of England, where Locke played an important role. And of course, the Glorious Revolution was no revolution at all; it was a military coup, whereby the base of the new Venetian-created Empire was shifted from Amsterdam to London.

Much more will be said about these events later in this work, but for now we will look at Locke's own words. I include fairly lengthy quotations from Locke,[39] because I think that is the best way for the reader to judge if these quotations reflect someone who could have even remotely influenced the United States Declaration of Independence and U.S. Constitution.

The Two Treatises of Government - This work is Locke's hymn to private property. He says:

> "Man has individual property in his own person. The
> labor of HIS body and the work of HIS hands allows
> him to remove from nature things which he can join
> to his own and make HIS property.
> "This the taking of any part of what is common,
> and removing it out of the state Nature leaves it in,
> which BEGINS THE PROPERTY; without which, the

---

[39] In the Locke quotations, all emphases are in the original

Common is of no use. And the taking of this or that part does not depend on the express consent of all the Commoners.

"The great and CHIEF END therefore, of Mens uniting into Commonwealths, and putting themselves under Government, IS THE PRESERVATION OF THEIR PROPERTY.

"PERSONS are FREE by a Native Right, and their PROPERTIES are THEIR OWN, AND AT THEIR OWN DISPOSE... Can (the King) take away the Goods or Money they have got upon the Land, at his pleasure? If he can, then all free and voluntary CONTRACTS cease, and are void, in the world."

Perhaps the most rabid quote is the following:

"The Reason why Men enter into Society, is the *preservation of their Property*; and the end why they chuse and authorize a Legislative, is, that there may be Laws made, and Rules set as Guards and Fences to the Properties of all Members of Society, to limit the Power and moderate the Dominion of every Part and Member of Society. For since it can never be supposed to be the Will of the Society, that the Legislative should have the Power to destroy that, which everyone designs to secure, by entering into Society, and for which the People submitted themselves to the Legislators of their own making; whenever the Legislators ENDEAVOR TO TAKE AWAY, AND DESTROY THE PROPERTY OF THE PEOPLE, or to reduce them to Slavery under Arbitrary Power, they put themselves into a State of War with the People, who are thereupon absolved from any further Obedience."

Slavery is merely the lawful epitome of these property rights:

"There is another sort of Servants, which by a peculiar Name, we call SLAVES, who being Captives taken in a Just War, are by the Right of Nature subjugated to the Absolute Dominion and Arbitrary Power of their Masters. These Men having, as I say, forfeited their Lives, and with it their Liberties, and lost their Estates; and being in the STATE OF SLAVERY, not capable of any property, cannot in that state be considered as any part of CIVIL SOCIETY; the chief end whereof is the preservation of PROPERTY."

In his *Fundamental Constitution of Carolina*, Locke wrote, "Every freeman shall have absolute power and authority over his negro slaves," and in his 1698 Instructions to Governor Nicholson of Virginia, Locke defended the African slave raids of the Royal Africa Company as "just wars." Locke states that in a "just war," the conqueror gains absolute despotic control over the vanquished.

A true irony is that, in Locke – the supposed inspiration for the American Revolution – *the notion of freedom he propounds is lifted directly from the theories of Roman Law.* Locke states that man's natural freedom derives from his original existence in a state of nature, a state of perfect freedom. Locke's notion of "all men created equal" is nothing but the Roman idea that all beasts are created free and equal in a state of nature. In this state, man – the beast – has the right to defend his life, liberty and possessions.

Men have the right to kill those who would violate this law of nature. Man surrenders some of his rights to enter society and to establish laws and courts (i.e., the Social Contract), but the fundamental law of nature prevails, and individual man retains his sovereignty. Created governments function only as arbiters (umpires) between sovereign individuals. Man enters into society only for the purpose of "the preservation of property of all the members of society, as far as possible." Private property rights existed BEFORE the creation of the state, and the role of the state is to protect this property.

Locke's idea of the "accession" of property entails a bizarre interpretation of the Book of Genesis, which virtually reduces the Supreme Being to the role of a vulture capitalist:

John Locke

"At the beginning of mankind's existence, 'the Law man was under, was rather for APPROPRIATING. God Commanded, and his wants forced him to LABOUR. That was his PROPERTY which could not be taken from him where-ever he had fixed it. And hence subduing or cultivating the Earth, and having Dominion, we see are joined together. The one gave Title to the other. So that God, by commanding to subdue, gave Authority so far to APPROPRIATE... (which) necessarily introduces PRIVATE POSSESSIONS.'"

<u>Some Considerations of the Consequences of the Lowering of Interest and Raising the Value of Money</u> –

In this work Locke goes beyond simple physical property rights and raises the issue of money itself, as a "special" kind of property, one imbued with almost magical powers. In arguing for what he calls "the natural interest of money," he says that money "turns the wheels of trade," therefore its course should not be stopped. This Lockean near-worship of the creature "money," occurred, of course, in the context of the creation of the Bank of England, and the importation of the financial speculative practices of Amsterdam into London. This rabid monetarism, in which money is given an intrinsic value of its own, as opposed to the Hamiltonian idea of Public Credit, where money and credit are merely tools by which sovereign economic development can be realized, is, today, unfortunately widespread, particularly among the "invisible hand" crowd in Vienna and Chicago. Once again, it should be pointed out, that in his writings on money, Locke is the cheap knock-off copy. All of what he says can be found in the Salamancan Navarrus.

Parliamentary Rule: Government by the Oligarchy

Many Europeans today are proud of their democracies or parliaments, but the unavoidable reality is that, although some individual European leaders have acted courageously as true patriots, no European nation has ever been a truly sovereign republic. The reason for this lies in the subjects we have already been considering. In the writings of Althusius, Mornay, Locke and others, it is explicit that oligarchical property rights, including "financial property" are beyond the reach of the civilian government. The apex of this practice is today's European system of private

Central Banking, acting outside of, and above government.

Or as the Salamancan de Menchaca said, more than a century before Locke: the state has the right of *dominium jurisdictions* (a limited jurisdiction to punish crime), but not *dominium proprietatis* (the right of ownership, the right of sovereignty).

In examining the role of civil government in the *Two Treatises*, John Locke puts it this way:

> "The first and fundamental Positive Law of all Commonwealths, is the establishing of the Legislative Power; as the First and Fundamental Natural Law... is the Preservation of the Society, and of every person in it. This Legislative is not only the Supreme Power of the Commonwealth, but sacred and unalterable in the hands where the Community have placed it."
>
> but... "The Supreme Power cannot take from any Man any part of his Property without his own consent. For the preservation of Property being the end of Government."

It is no accident that for Locke and his many predecessors, the examples of Sparta, and particularly Venice, are proclaimed as the model for Parliamentary rule.

So the defining issue between Europe and America is not about the form of our legislative institutions, it is about the issue of *Sovereignty*. Parliamentary governments are designed to be subordinate creatures of a financial oligarchy. Let me repeat: all Parliamentary systems are intended to be weak systems of limited sovereignty. In contrast, a Commonwealth embodies the sovereign principle, as Abraham Lincoln put it, of government "of the people, by the people, and for the people." In such a sovereign nation there is no other unreachable power allowed above that sovereignty.

Algernon Sidney – Sidney, who lived at the same time as Locke, was not a particularly important person. However, the manner in which the "myth of Algernon Sidney" was used to consolidate the modern form of British Parliamentary government, in the years following the 1688 Glorious Revolution, is important, and worth describing. Sidney was the grand-nephew of the famous Philip Sidney. As a teenager he lived for four years in Paris, where he came under the influence of Hugo Grotius, who was a close friend of his father in the Mersenne Circle. Sidney later said of Grotius' *Law of War and Peace*, that it was the most important book ever written on political theory.[40]

Sidney spent most of his adult life as a political exile on the Continent, where, among other things, he established a close relationship with the Dutch leader Johann DeWitt. During this period, and after his return to England in 1677, he came under the influence of both the English Ambassador William Temple and John Locke's employer, Anthony Ashley Cooper (the Earl of Shaftesbury.). Temple and Cooper were at the center of conspiratorial efforts to effect a Dutch invasion and coup in England. Acting on their behalf, in 1666, Sidney proposed to DeWitt that he launch an invasion of England for the purpose of restoring Parliamentary rule. Later, in 1679, William Temple sent Algernon's brother Henry back to the Netherlands in another failed attempt to get the Dutch to invade, this time offering the English crown to William of Orange. In 1682, Algernon Sidney was arrested for his alleged involvement in the "Rye House Plot" against King Charles II, and, ultimately, he was executed along with several others,

---

[40] *Memoirs of Algernon Sydney,* by George Wilson Meadley, printed by Thomas Davison, 1813

including Lord William Russell.

After the eventual, and successful, Dutch invasion of 1688, Sidney was hailed as a national hero. One of the first acts of the new King William III was to sign into law an act overturning the convictions of Sidney and Russell. This occurred almost simultaneous with Parliament passing, and William signing, the *Declaration of Rights*, which many historians point to as the document which established the permanency of parliamentary rule in Britain. The *Declaration* was written by Sidney's close friend Lord John Somers, and modeled directly on Sidney's *Discourses*.[41] Sidney was lionized by the Whig leaders as the martyr of the parliamentary cause. Several editions of the *Discourses* were published, and a cult of Algernon Sidney was propagated throughout the English-speaking world.[42]

In reality, the nature of Sidney's republicanism is revealed by his close relationship with the head of the Dutch Empire Johan DeWitt. Additionally, in the *Discourses*, Sidney is effusive in his praise for John Locke. He also argues aggressively in favor of rule by an aristocracy,

Algernon Sidney

and, like Locke, his defense of property rights is explicit.[43]

---

[41] *Discourses Concerning Government,* Sidney's main published work

[42] The adulation of Sidney was such that aristocrats began naming their children Sidney or Sydney, which had previously been only a surname.

[43] A revealing glimpse into the fakery of Sidney's "republicanism" is his close association with the Englishman Henry Vane. In 1637 Vane had been expelled by John Winthrop from the Massachusetts Bay Colony, for his attempts to disrupt the government of that actual Commonwealth.

The best yardstick to judge Sidney is to look at the events of 1688. The *Invitation to William*, the document asking William of Orange to invade England, was authored by Henry Sidney, Algernon's brother. Among the signers of the *Invitation* (the "Immortal Seven"), three of the seven were: Henry Sidney (later William III's First Lord of the Admiralty), Edward Russell (the cousin of William Russell, and later a member of William III's Privy Council), and William Cavendish, of the famous Cavendish clan. And of course, when the Dutch invasion fleet arrived in England, one of the passengers was John Locke, returning to England to continue the work of his now-deceased employer, Anthony Ashley Cooper, the Earl of Shaftesbury.

A brief note on the Malthusians

From ancient times to today's 21st century, a core feature of the Empire's hatred of humanity is what we would call today Malthusianism. Humanity is to be controlled, looted, exploited, and, if necessary, killed to maintain the Empire. From the standpoint of a Venetian Doge, or today's Prince Philip Mountbatten, the human species needs to be culled from time to time.

In the post-1582 era, the birth of an explicitly Malthusian doctrine has had the Empire's DNA imprinted on it from the very beginning. One of the first to attack the Empire's population "problem" was the Jesuit Giovanni Botero. Botero can best be described as "in the Salamanca orbit." In his 1589 work *Ragione di Stato*, where Botero argues that the best way to secure the public welfare is through free market forces, he states that his views are deeply indebted to the work of the Salamancans Francisco de Vitoria and Domingo de Soto. This idea, that the Common Good is best served by free market financial and economic policies, is, as we have already seen, a subversion of Cusa's Commonwealth idea. Later, in his *Delle cause della grandezza e magnificenze della città*, Botero deals directly with the problem of poverty and population, and, like Malthus later, he ascribes the widespread urban poverty and misery to overpopulation and a lack of resources. This work was acclaimed by the influential Salamancan Lessius, who became a public supporter of Botero. Later, this same work would have a powerful influence over William Petty and Edmund Halley after its translation into English and 1606 publication in London.

In 1647, a Genoese aristocrat named Giovanni Battista Baliani, a friend and correspondent of Galileo, published *Trattato della Pestilenza*, a treatise on the plague. In discussing the cause of the plague, he writes, "For it is impossible to go on always filling the world with more and more without many persons dying of hunger for the earth cannot feed a great many more than are living at present... This evil, however deplorable, is inevitable. It is therefore necessary that so great a number of people will from time to time be diminished." Baliani sent the work to Marin Mersenne in Paris. Mersenne published it and established an ongoing correspondence with Baliani.

Beginning in the 1670s we find the writings of DeWitt, John Graunt, Edmund Halley, and Francis Bacon's protege William Petty on demographics, all of a linear statistical Malthusian nature, and in the 18th century the work of the Venetian aristocrat Giammaria Ortes, which was plagiarized by Thomas Malthus himself.

All of this was designed to justify the poverty and human suffering that resulted from the financial and economic looting of the Empire, in exactly the same way as modern-day Malthusians like Paul Erlich and Al Gore[44] have justified the economic looting and genocide under our current regime of globalization.

VII. The new Venice in Amsterdam

Wisselbank in Amsterdam

The tragedy of the Netherlands, and perhaps the lesson for our own United States today, is that its oligarchical future was built over the ashes of a destroyed humanist past. The home of Jan Van Eyck, the Brethren of the Common Life, and Erasmus, it is often said that the Florentine Renaissance had more of an impact on the Low Countries than anywhere else outside of Italy. How did the Venetians turn this place of great culture into the new seat of Empire? The answer is terror—almost 100 years of war, Inquisition and barbarism beyond anything people today can imagine. History is too often presented as if it did not contain real human beings. To understand what happened in the Netherlands, one must first understand what was done to the Dutch and Flemish people.[45]

In the 1520s, the Netherlands, which then included what are today Belgium and Luxembourg, were under Spanish-Hapsburg rule. The first public burning of a Protestant heretic occurred in 1523, and by the 1530s hundreds were being executed. In 1567 the infamous Duke of Alva arrived with 10,000 Spanish troops, both to enforce the Inquisition, and to impose a regime of massive economic looting to extract money which the Spanish Crown owed to its Fugger creditors. Alva created a royal tribunal known as the Council of Blood which over a six year span executed more than 12,000 people. In addition to the executions,

---

[45] See Friedrich Schiller's *History of the Revolt of the Netherlands*

Alva conducted military campaigns to subjugate the Dutch people. In his campaign of 1572 major cities such as Mechlin, Zutphen and Haarlem were captured, looted and burnt to the ground, with the populations either exterminated or delivered over to rape and torture. In the Spanish Fury of 1576, the Netherlands' premier city Antwerp was occupied, and over 8,000 civilians were slaughtered, with hacked, mutilated, naked, and burnt bodies left lying in the streets

There were two responses to this carnage. The Dutch leader William the Silent led a war of national liberation against the Spanish. His supporters included Dutch Catholics, Lutherans and Calvinists, and his policy was one of religious toleration.[46] But at the same time, the population was being driven insane by the decades of the Spanish horrors, creating a recruiting ground for the radical Calvinists. Friends of Venice, Phillipe du Plessis-Mornay and Hubert Languet, were both very active in the Netherlands during this period. After William's assassination by a Jesuit agent in 1584, all hope for an ecumenical peace evaporated. William's death resulted in the rapid ascendancy of the most rabid of the Calvinists, including his son Maurice of Nassau. The forces of the Calvinists and the House of Orange merged, and their rallying cry became the Union of *"Kerk en Oranje"* (Church and Orange). This is the grouping which would bring the Netherlands into a military alliance with Paolo Sarpi's Venice by 1610. This is the same grouping which in 1621 created the Dutch West India Company, and seized control of much of the African slave trade from the Spanish and Portuguese.

---

[46] As seen in the 1579 Union of Utrecht, which at William's insistence, contained a clause (Article 13) guaranteeing liberty of conscience in religious worship, and prohibiting the persecution of anyone for religious reasons.

Creating the new Venice

In the 26 years between the murder of William the Silent and the establishment of the Dutch-Venetian alliance, a new generation came to power in the Netherlands. With this new leadership, the hope for a Dutch republic ended, and the Netherlands was taken in a new direction, increasingly steered by the economic and financial colossus emerging in Amsterdam. Prior to the Dutch Wars of Liberation, Amsterdam had been a moderately successful commercial city for centuries, trading in herring, wool and other commodities. After the

William the Silent

Spanish occupation of Antwerp in 1585, Amsterdam would become the new financial capital of the nation.

Earlier, during the mid-sixteenth century, Antwerp had been the financial and banking center of all northern Europe, and even rivaled Venice, Genoa, and Augsburg as the preeminent financial center in all of Europe. Antwerp was the "money market of the world" – "the "Venice of the North" – and 5,000 merchants from every nation had their representatives at the *Bourse* (stock exchange). The Venetian-controlled German House of Fugger, together with the Genoese banks, were the dominant foreign financial interests in the city.

After the destruction of Antwerp, thousands of people fled north, and many of Antwerp's bankers, speculators, and merchants relocated to Amsterdam. These emigrants included Jan de Wael, Jacob Poppin, and Isaac Le Maire, all of whom would play a major role in the founding of the Dutch East India Company. The creation of the financial center in Amsterdam also entailed the emergence of a new elite. Of the ten wealthiest families in Amsterdam in 1550, none remained among the ten wealthiest by 1600.

No time was lost in creating a new maritime/financial capital in Amsterdam. In 1594, the Dutch "Long Distance Company" was founded, beginning trade with Asia. In 1600, the first Dutch ships reached Japan. In 1601, the East India Company (VOC) was founded. Its founder Johan van Oldenbarneveldt said: "The great East India Company, with 4 years of hard work public and private, I have helped establish, in order to inflict damage on the Spanish and Portuguese." In 1605, the Dutch began their takeover of Indonesia, which they would not relinquish for almost 350 years. 1606 saw the first known voyage of Dutch slave ships. In 1608, the New Bourse was opened in Amsterdam, to replace the Antwerp exchange. In 1609, the Bank of Amsterdam (*Wisselbank*) was founded, modeled on the practices of the Bank of Venice. Later that same year, the Treaty of Antwerp was signed, whereby the Spanish officially recognized Dutch independence. It was Venice that had the distinction of being the first government in Europe to recognize Dutch independence, and it was Venice that was the first government to which the Dutch sent an ambassador.

VOC – the United East India Company

The Dutch East India Company created the greatest maritime empire the world had ever seen, and it was not until the late 18th century that the British East India

Company surpassed it. The VOC dominated Asia trade for almost 2 centuries. To compare, consider that between 1602 to 1795, the VOC sent 4,785 ships to Asia, and carried more than 2.5 million tons of Asian goods. During the same period, the British East India Company sent 2,650 ships, and carried only 500,000 tons of goods. The Dutch began their empire by either destroying or taking over almost all of the Portuguese colonies in Asia. From there, they moved on to seizing new ones. The Christian Dutch methods were beyond brutal. In 1621, for example, the natives of the Island of Band refused to give the Dutch a nutmeg monopoly. In response the VOC Governor General Jan Pieterszoon gave orders to kill the entire native population. The order was carried out, the population was exterminated, and slaves brought in to work the Dutch plantations.

As already reported earlier in this work, this was a *private* empire. The colonies, the military fortresses, the slaves, and all of the loot extracted, belonged to the VOC and its investors, not to the Dutch government. The VOC had its own army and navy. All of the military personnel were recruited and armed by the VOC and served under VOC command.

The VOC made Batavia (today's Jakarta) the capital of their Asian empire, headed by a Governor-General and assisted by a "Council of the Indies." All of the Dutch eastern colonies were ruled from Batavia, except for those in Persia, India, Ceylon, and South Africa, which received orders directly from the VOC, itself, in Amsterdam.

The Bank & the Bourse

The New Bourse (exchange) opened in Amsterdam in 1608, and the Bank of Amsterdam (*Wisselbank*) followed the next year. The *Wisselbank* was, like the Bank of Venice, a *privately owned public bank*; i.e., it had a monopoly on all exchange of specie, and trade in precious metals; it was a clearinghouse for bills of exchange; and it handled the debt of the Dutch government. It was *public* in the sense that it assumed the sovereign power to dictate financial policies, and those policies became the nation's policies. The Bank's directors had offices in City Hall, and its money was kept in the city vault. The security of its holdings established the new "bank money" as the center of the city's securities trading. This, combined with the international trade in hard currency (specie), made Amsterdam the world's largest international securities market (including VOC company paper and municipal bonds). The most popular of the securities investments was the national debt.

But it was *privately owned!* And, as in Venice, this arrangement represented the handing over of sovereign control over economic and monetary policy to an oligarchical elite. In effect the financial oligarchy simply swallowed the sovereign institutions of government.

It is necessary here, however, to clarify a key point. The pivotal issue is not the role of private investors, *per se*. This is the reductionist error made by those who criticize the role of private investors in Alexander Hamilton's Bank of the United States. The issue is not "public versus private." The core defining issue is one of sovereignty. The Venetian model of empire is one of national subservience to a primarily internationalist financial empire. Private investors in a national bank which is constitutionally deployed to fund the technological, scientific and industrial development of the nation is not the same thing. Don't think like an empiricist; think, instead, of *intention*.

The Amsterdam Bourse was modeled directly on the earlier Antwerp Bourse. As was to be the relationship between the London Stock Exchange and the British East India Company a century later, the initial activity of the Bourse was centered in speculation on the shares of the VOC. After 1612 a secondary market was created, for shares and futures, and capitalization of the VOC became permanent.

The trading in financial securities, which took place at the Bourse, created the first modern stock exchange, and by the mid-1600s, the Amsterdam Bourse was described as the "place where the whole world trades."[47] During the 17th century there was a famous boast about the Amsterdam Bourse which was printed on plaques, posters, and medallions:

Ephesus fame was her temple
Tyre her market and port
Babylon her masonry walls
Memphis her pyramids
Rome her empire
All the world praises me

By 1621, all of the institutions of the modern oligarchical state were in place in the Netherlands. If you look at what was created, in terms of the institutions, the accumulation of capital, and the capability to deploy that capital on behalf of the Empire, the scope of the accomplishment is actually breathtaking. The practices of the Bank, the Bourse, and the VOC, were all Venetian in origin, but the sheer size and power of the new financial, political, and military capabilities involved was beyond anything seen before.

As in Venice, and later in London, an oligarchical system produces an oligarchical culture. The Dutch Empire, based

---

[47] This revolution in financial practices which took place at the Bourse will be examined more thoroughly in Chapter 9

on looting, speculation, and slavery was no exception. By 1630, almost all of the wealthier classes were involved in the East India trade, or finance speculation, or both, and by 1650 the Netherlands had been transformed largely into a rentier economy. Anyone who has ever visited Amsterdam's *Riksmuseum* cannot help but be struck by the observation that most of the paintings that are contemporary with Rembrandt are horrible—romantic/stoic cartoons of petty oligarchs and Regents. Rembrandt, who knew the evil within which he existed, spent most of his adult life being persecuted by the Dutch establishment.

Huge mansions and villas were constructed for the Dutch elite on the banks of the river Vecht. Constantin Huygens, an agent of the House of Orange, wrote his most famous poem, *Batavia's Temple*, celebrating the new mansion he was building. This was truly a recreation of the Venetian oligarchy, just as, centuries later, the plantation owners of the American South would try to recreate the world of the English gentry. Perhaps the best description of this decayed corrupt culture is presented (admiringly) in Bernard de Mandeville's *Fable of the Bees*:

"What made that contemptible spot of earth so considerable among the powers of Europe has been their political wisdom in postponing everything to merchandise and navigation... In pictures and marble they are profuse; in their buildings and gardens they are extravagant to folly. In other countries you meet with stately courts and palaces which nobody can expect in a commonwealth, but in all Europe you shall find no private buildings so sumptuously magnificent as a great many of the merchants' and other gentlemen's houses are in Amsterdam and in some of the great cities of that small province."

Oldenbarneveldt & Grotius

Much has been written, and many praises have been sung, about the "republican" nature of the Dutch Empire. Most of this incompetent and idiotic foolishness points to two periods in Dutch history: the government of Johan van Oldenbarneveldt from 1587 to 1618, and the government of Johann De Witt from 1653 to 1672. Once again, these historical lies result from the inability of the historians to distinguish between a society governed by the principles of Empire versus the mission of a sovereign Commonwealth.

As the Advocate of Holland for more than 30 years, Oldenbarneveldt was the most powerful political official in the Netherlands. He was the founder

Johan van Oldenbarneveldt

of the Dutch East India Company, and it was under his leadership that the Venetian system was recreated in Amsterdam. In 1613 Oldenbarneveldt named his protégé, Hugo Grotius, to the post of Pensionary of Holland, the second most powerful political post in the government. It was under the leadership of Oldenbarneveldt and Grotius that the Dutch Empire was created, and the alliance with Venice was realized. Oldenbarneveldt went so far as to send his own son as the first Dutch ambassador to Venice.

The problem came on the eve of the Thirty Years War, in 1618, as the Netherlands's 12 year truce with Spain was about to expire. Oldenbarneveldt wanted to extend the truce. Venice wanted European wide war. The Venetians provoked a conflict between Oldenbarneveldt and the House of Orange, which ultimately resulted in a military takeover by Maurice of Nassau, the arrest and execution of Oldenbarneveldt and the imprisonment of Grotius. Standard histories attribute the downfall of Oldenbarneveldt to his opposition to the radical Calvinists. This is known as the Remonstrant controversy (the "Arminius versus Gomarus" theological conflict). The truth is, Venice wanted the Orangist War Party in power.[48] Oldenbarneveldt's ouster was indispensable if Venice's plans for European War were to proceed. After Oldenbarneveldt's downfall, the Dutch Stadholder Maurice seized absolute power, signed a military alliance with Venice, and reopened the war with Spain.

Hobbesian Freedom

For the next thirty-two years the Netherlands was under the direct rule of the House of Orange, but in 1650 the Stadtholder (essentially Prince) William II died at a young age, with no successors. This initiated a 21 year period of civilian rule that came to be known as "True Freedom." This period is synonymous with the name Johan DeWitt, who from 1653 to 1672 served as the Grand Pensionary of Holland, and who, together with his brother Cornelis, effectively ran the Dutch government.

Many historians proclaim the DeWitt era as the model of Dutch republicanism, some even going so far as to see in it

---

[48] This is explicit in a letter sent by Paolo Sarpi to Isaac Casaubon, praising the outcome of the Council of Dort, where the final decree condemned Oldenbarneveldt's Arminian allies, and supported the position of the Orangist Gomarists.

a precursor of the United States. Before one loses all bearings on reality, it is worth reminding one's self that it was under the DeWitts that the Dutch Empire reached the zenith of its power, including almost complete control of the African slave trade.

Actually, it is in this era of the DeWitt brothers, that we see the real model for the modern oligarchical state. This is the period of Micanzio's Mersenne Circle, and if there was one place on the planet where the oligarchical scientific and

Johan DeWitt

political theories of that Circle had their greatest impact, it was in the Netherlands of the DeWitts. The works of Descartes were spreading like wildfire through the Dutch universities, and Johann DeWitt went so far as to actually personally publish an edition of Descartes' *La Geometric*, with an introduction written by himself. DeWitt also authored perhaps the first major work on demographics and insurance. His *Value of Life Annuities in Proportion to Redeemable Bonds*, pioneered the concept of calculating the value of a human life, as determined by the mathematical expectation of dying.[49]

Guiding the philosophy and policies of the Dutch state, during this period, was a second set of brothers, Johann and Pieter de la Court. They were very close personally to the DeWitts, and they authored numerous works, including *Interest of Holland, Political Balance,* and *Political*

---

[49] *The Life and Times of John DeWitt,* by Robert Barnwell, Pudney & Russell, New York, 1856

Discourses. After Johann's death in 1660, Pieter became the leading influence in DeWitt's government. The De la Courts were total products of the Mersenne curriculum. In *Political Balance* they write, "Descartes and Hobbes show the way to the theory that should occupy mankind, as he was and not as the old-fashioned professors chose to see him." In the *Political Discourses*, they say, "The natural state is the Hobbesian unrestrained state of nature; the best state exists where the unreasonable passions are most restrained. That is the democratic republic." That pessimistic view of the human condition is further underscored by Johann, who wrote, "Only in the private, inner, domestic circle can one rest from the struggle of an antagonistic world." Johann was a passionate admirer of both Venice and Genoa, and he said "Unqualified and mean persons should have nothing to do with government and administration which must be reserved for qualified people alone."

The de la Court brothers envisioned a "civic republic" based on the extreme Hobbesian view of individual passions. Each individual can be viewed as an atom impelled by passion through the void of society. Order is achieved by controlling the continual collisions that occur between such heteronomic individuals. What is remarkable, if not surprising, is the coherence between Sarpi's philosophical empiricism, and the development of a Hobbesian social theory based on individual passions and property rights. Man exists in a purposeless atomistic universe of material objects, and he defines himself by his possession of those objects.

The DeWitts ultimately met the same fate as Oldenbarneveldt at the hands of the House of Orange, but only *naiveté* or deliberate fraud could lead one to profess their Empire as a forerunner of the American republic.

The Empire

When the Treaty of Westphalia was signed in 1648, the Dutch Empire was the greatest power in the world, and Amsterdam was the financial capital of Europe. The Dutch dominated the African slave trade. They had a stranglehold on international trade in specie, sugar, spices, and furs, and in the 1640s and 1650s, they finished off the Portuguese in Asia. In 1641 the Dutch established a monopoly on trade with Japan which lasted until 1853, and in 1661 Portugal submitted to a treaty granting the Dutch complete free trade, and the right of Dutch citizens to settle in any Portuguese territory.

The imperial apex came with the Second Anglo-Dutch War (1665-1667), which ended in the defeat of England, and with the Dutch fleet sailing up the Thames. From the flagship of that fleet, the Dutch dictated the terms of the peace treaty.

The Dutch Empire seemed invincible, but in reality, a much more powerful evil was soon to arise.

In 1672, a coalition of European nations combined to attack the Netherlands. The Dutch suffered a devastating and total defeat, with the French armies of Louis XIV occupying whole sections of their country. Dutch historians refer to 1672 as the "Year of Disaster." The defeat led to the collapse of the DeWitt government, and the execution of the two brothers. The House of Orange was returned to power, in the form of the young Prince William III, but the geographical and military vulnerabilities of the Netherlands were exposed for all to see.

Once the war was settled, and the House of Orange consolidated its position, Venetian networks on both sides of the North Sea, began to plot the next, more powerful, phase of Empire. This would entail not another Dutch war against England, but rather the complete takeover of the British Isles and the merger of England into a new joint Anglo-Dutch Empire. In 1678, a marriage was arranged between the Dutch Prince William and Mary, the daughter of King James II, and the first in line of succession to the English throne. The very next year Henry Sidney was at William's court in the The Hague, offering him the English throne and asking him to invade England and seize the government. Sidney returned to the Hague as the English Ambassador in 1681, and during the next few years, the negotiations for a Dutch takeover continued and intensified. Then came 1688, and the Anglo-Dutch Empire was born.

VIII. Money, Speculation & Gambling

Gamblers at the Ridotto

"If one were to lead a stranger through the streets of Amsterdam and ask him where he was, he would answer 'Among speculators,' for there is no corner in the city where one does not talk shares."

Joseph de la Vega, in *Confusion de Confusiones,* 1688[50]

Today, as the bankruptcy of our current financial system becomes more and more apparent, a growing number of critics have attacked what they call the "transformation of our financial system into a casino economy." Many counterpose the recent binge of financial speculation and the excesses of globalization to what they profess is the "normal" functioning of the financial markets and the economy. But they are wrong. The speculation, the economic looting, and the spread of slave labor are the nature of the Empire, and its modern representation in the British system of Free Trade.

What makes people think we had a "normal economy" in the 1950s and 1960s, is that we had Franklin Roosevelt 20 years earlier. And it was Roosevelt's revival of the anti-empire outlook of Alexander Hamilton, and FDR's regulatory measures such as the Glass-Steagall Act, which kept the Empire at bay until 1971. There is either the

---

[50] *Confusion de Confusiones,* by Joseph de la Vega (1688), the Kress Library, Harvard University, 1957

Empire or the American system. There is no "normal economy" at some vague location in-between.

Originating in Venice, and aided by the works of the Salamancans, among others, during the 17th century, the oligarchy initiated a vast revolution in financial policy. We have already looked at a few of those institutional changes. Here we will look at some of the content, to get at the essence of the insane oligarchical view of what constitutes wealth. We have already touched on the creation of the radical notion of "property rights" and the invention of the insane magical notion of "money" as creations of the oligarchy. Here we will look at these matters a little bit further, and how they were used to create the functional institutions of the Empire.

Antwerp – the Laboratory

The Antwerp Bourse opened in 1531. Initially, most of the financial contracts were tied to trading in hard commodities, like wool, in a manner not dissimilar to the earlier famous Champagne Fairs. But as time went on, the activity of the Bourse was shifted over to almost entirely purely speculative investments. This transformation included the invention of new financial instruments such as futures contracts and other forms of financial derivatives. Later, in Amsterdam, these Antwerp innovations would be taken much, much further.[51]

One of the Antwerp innovations was that Bills of Exchanges, which had already existed in Venice, Genoa and other locations, were made transferable. This led to the practice of discounting Bills, and the development of a speculative money market in short term paper. Two

---

[51] *Amsterdam as the cradle of modern futures and options trading,* by Oscar Gelderblom and Joost Jonker, Utrecht University

Imperial edicts gave legal protection on the negotiability of these notes.

It was in Antwerp, also, that "futures trading" (a claim on the price of a commodity or security transaction to occur at some future date) became commonplace. A limited use of primitive futures contracts had already been used at the commercial fairs of the 15th and 16th centuries, but it was at Antwerp that speculation in futures became routine. It was at Antwerp, as well, that "option contracts" (the right to speculate on something you don't actually own) were invented. Later, after 1600, options trading was to become

The Antwerp Bourse

a dominant practice of the Amsterdam market. This Antwerp/Amsterdam creation of options contracts was the mother of all of the purely financial derivatives trading that occurs today.

By the 1570s, investments at the Antwerp Bourse were almost entirely centered in purely speculative financial contracts. Speculators also gambled on the rise and fall of currency exchange rates. A Bill of Exchange, drawn at Antwerp was the most common commercial currency in Europe.

All of this activity was premised on an oligarchical-created notion that wealth is defined by money, and that the markets were a way of creating or stealing this wealth out of thin air. Money and other financial instruments, which somehow seemed to magically exist in a free marketplace, held the power to excite and enrich anyone clever enough to possess them. Completely absent of course, was the Commonwealth idea that real wealth stems from the deliberate fostering of the creative capabilities of the individual human members of society, and the power of those individuals to develop new inventions and discoveries which can transform and truly enrich man's relationship with the universe.

Banking & Money

Although the Antwerp Bourse was the testing ground for many of the financial practices later adopted in Amsterdam, it was also merely a financial exchange, located within the Hapsburg domains. Amsterdam, conversely, was destined to become the financial capital of a maritime empire, and the place where the true implications of the Venetian-inspired Anglo-Dutch model could be realized.

Antwerp had the Bourse; Amsterdam had the Dutch East India Company, the Amsterdam Exchange, and the Bank of Amsterdam, and it was in Amsterdam that our current modern form of European Central Banking was created.

From a technical standpoint, the single most important banking invention in Amsterdam was that of *Central Bank*

Money,[52] which is often described as the foundation of modern central banking systems. This developed around the notion of a "unit of account," establishing a relationship of bank money (the privately issued notes of the bank) to specie, with the value of the bank money eventually becoming the actual legal unit of account and the basis for the final settlement of all contracts and accounts. When the *Wisselbank* ended the right of specie withdrawal in the 1680s, the ascendancy of fiat bank money was complete. The financial paper of the Central Bank was legally, the official money of the realm, so to speak.

What this did was to institutionalize a system whereby the power of money replaced any concept of the Common Good as the governing principle of society. It also took the power over currency and credit out of the hands of the sovereign government. The issues involved here are not technical; they are axiomatic. This concept of the pre-eminence of money is at the heart of the modern System of Central Banking. It is a system based on money, usury, and debt, where both the people, as well as the government, are controlled through the Central Bank's power over money and debt. The purpose of the debt is not to finance physical economic development for the benefit of the Common Good, but to perpetuate the wealth and governing power of the financial oligarchy.

By the second half of the 17th century, the *Wisselbank* had amassed an enormous concentration of financial power, which gave them the ability to expand the Empire and finance wars on a scale never before seen.

---

[52] *The Bank of Amsterdam and the Leap to Central Bank Money,* by Stephen Quinn and William Roberds

Speculating

The center of the new Empire's activity in financial speculation was the Amsterdam Bourse. The Bourse was a money market, a finance market, and a stock market. Practices included futures, options, margin loans, financial leverage, speculation in foreign securities, and trading in outright derivatives (known as *ductions*).

Options trading did not become a widespread financial practice in Amsterdam until the 1630s, and its emergence was connected directly to the dividend policy of the VOC. From 1603 to 1620, the VOC only paid dividends to shareholders three times, but by 1635 they began paying yearly dividends, with annual returns ranging from 15 to 65 percent. These yearly dividends then became the basis for widespread betting (options) on what they would eventually be worth.

To clarify matters, the difference between the three main types of contracts traded at the Amsterdam Bourse is as follows:

- **Forward contract**: an obligation to take delivery of a commodity at a specific date, at a fixed price. (this can be a physical commodity or a financial instrument)

- **Futures contract**: essentially a transferable Forward contract, where the original buyer may sell his claim, turning the contract into a tradable asset.

- **Options contract**: the *right* (not obligation) to sell or buy a contract at a specific date, at an agreed price. This allowed investors to take market positions at a fraction of the cost. These were also transferable.

By 1650, a 21st century-style market in options trading, including "puts" (*prime a recevoir*) and "calls" (*prime a delivrer*), was widespread. One historian has called it a "mature speculative market." The Tulipmania of 1637-1638 was based almost entirely on futures and options trading, and by 1688, a full-blown derivatives market existed in Amsterdam. Many of these Dutch practices were later imported into London in the 1690s.

In 1688, an eyewitness account of the Amsterdam speculative market was published under the title of *Confusion de Confusiones*. Written in Spanish, it was the work of Joseph de la Vega, a Sephardic Jew. The work is a series of four dialogues between a Merchant, a Philosopher, and a Speculator, and, in it, De la Vega describes in detail the various types of transactions on the Amsterdam market, including:

1.   Cash purchases and sales of real stock
2.   Margin sales, where the buyer puts up only 20 percent
3.   Futures contracts
4.   Options trading
5.   "Duction Shares" - speculating on the performance of the market or individual shares, without actually owning anything. Duction shares were purely fictitious, gambling on the future course of the market.

In De la Vega's account, the philosophy of the Amsterdam market is given by the Speculator, in the first dialogue, where he says:

"The best and most agreeable aspect of the new

business is that one can become rich without risk, indeed without endangering your capital."

Fisher Black and Myron Scholes could not have said it better.[53]

Gambling

In 1638, simultaneous with the creation of the Amsterdam speculative market, the first government-sponsored gambling casino in European history opened in Venice—the famous *Ridotto*.

Not surprisingly, Venice had been the center of European gambling[54] since at least the 13th century. In 1229, the election of a doge was determined by a throw of dice. Open gambling flourished during the Carnival season, which often lasted from October through March. During the 14th century the development of card games emerged first in Venice and spread from there to other cities. Venice also pioneered in the creation of private lotteries, which then were copied throughout Italy and in France and Flanders.

But it was casino gambling that made Venice unique. Casino gambling was invented in Venice. In fact, the word—*casino*—first appears in Venice. By the mid-16th century, numerous private gambling houses, known as *ridotti*, were operating throughout Venice. Towards the end of the century many of these *ridotti* had changed from places where individuals gambled against each other, to establishments where bettors played against the "house," the method still in use in present-day Las Vegas.

In 1638 the Venetian Grand Council voted to establish

---

[53] For more on the Black-Scholes Model for modern derivatives trading, see Chapter 13

[54] *Roll the Bones: The History of Gambling*, by David G. Schwartz, Gotham Books

the first government-owned gambling house in Europe. Known simply as the *Ridotto*, it was housed at the San Moise Palace which was owned by the Venetian nobleman Marco Dandolo, a descendant of the leader of the fourth crusade. At the *Ridotto*, aristocrats, prostitutes, pimps, usurers, degenerate gamblers, and many foreign visitors rubbed shoulders. All wore masks to protect their identity. In addition to the gambling, a room called the "Chamber of Sighs" provided a place for sexual liaisons.

More than a gambling hall, the *Ridotto* functioned as an ideal tool for the corruption and blackmail of foreign guests. Of the many thousands who frequented it's gaming tables, perhaps the two most famous were the Venetian spy Giacomo Casanova, and the speculator John Law. In 1768 the *Ridotto* was enlarged, using money confiscated from religious convents. In 1774 the Venetian Senate voted to close the Ridotto, after a large number of the Venetian nobility had gambled themselves into poverty. However, this only led to a proliferation of private casinos.

A great expansion of gambling took place in France during the reign of Louis XIV, when games like roulette, baccarat and blackjack became popular. During the Regency of Louis XV, when the finances of France were turned over to John Law, licensed gambling houses spread all over Paris, and of course, Law, himself, imported the gambling methods of the *Ridotto* into his manipulation of the finances of the French nation. Law spent his last years back in Venice, a regular at the gambling tables, and in 1729 he was buried in a plot of land adjacent to the *Ridotto*.

Theory

It should be obvious, at this point in the story, that the axiomatic nature of both the gambling at Venice's *Ridotto* and the financial speculation at the Amsterdam Bourse, are identical. They both rest on the idea that "wealth" is defined by that magical thing called money, and that the accumulation of wealth has no connection to any physical economic process. In methodology, they are also both based on the linear statistical mathematical methods introduced by Paolo Sarpi.

One of the first modern writings on gambling theory was *Sopra le Scoperte* ("Concerning an Investigation on Dice"), written by Sarpi's puppet Galileo Galilei. In this work, Galileo employs a method of statistical probability to attempt to determine the outcome (odds) of various combinations of a dice throw, using a set of three dice. During this formative period of the Anglo-Dutch financial system, two other major works on gambling theory also appeared. These were Girolamo Cardano's *Liber de Ludo Aleae* ("The Book on Games of Chance"), and *The Doctrine of Chances*, written by Abraham de Moivre.

These works, which have experienced a recent revival in popularity in our current era of unregulated hedge funds and derivatives trading, were all based on the idea that occurrences in the real world can be reduced to linear mathematical formulas. This methodology all comes from Sarpi, Galileo, and Descartes. Not only is it the basis for all of the financial "formulas" – like the infamous Black-Scholes Formula – used today in the speculative derivatives market, it also formed the basis for the oligarchical creation of modern insurance companies. And, of course it is the exact same method used today by professional card counters in Las Vegas and Atlantic City.[55]

These writings on gambling, particularly those of De Moivre, were also the theoretical foundation for the creation

---

[55] See *Yes! It Really is Gambling*, by Robert Ingraham

of the modern insurance industry.[56]   One of the earliest works in this field was the aforementioned *Value of Life Annuities in Proportion to Redeemable Bonds*, by the Dutch leader Johann DeWitt.   Additionally, between 1662 and 1724 a series of works were written by De Moivre, William Petty, Edmund Halley, and John Graunt. The mechanical-statistical method employed by all of these writers led into what we would call today modern probability theory.

Statistical probability theory, which is the basis for all financial speculation, gambling and the actuarial tables of the insurance industry comes from Sarpi's notion of empiricism and sense certainty. Sarpi says, that whether it be clamshells, dollar bills, or numbers, individual empirical data can be counted, and formulas can be devised to predict the outcome of any set of linear statistics. For Sarpi, this is the real world of the senses. *This is the opposite of Johannes Kepler's approach, that the real universe can only be understood through scientific investigation that leads towards discoveries of the actual non-linear underlying principles which bound the conduct of that universe.*

An example of the difference in the two approaches is the discovery of the calculus by Gottfried Leibniz, where he demonstrates that the calculus is a representation of a lawfully-ordered principle of creation, versus Isaac Newton's fraudulent calculus, based on a statistical approach, not dissimilar to earlier, failed, linear attempts to square the circle. In the real world, the concrete outcome of Sarpi's methodology, is the delusion that the financial markets can be used, predicted, and manipulated to amass more and more wealth (countable money), regardless of what is going on in the physical economy or the real state of the

---

[56] *From Commercial Arithmetic to Life Annuities: The Early History of Financial Economics,* 1478-1776, by Geoffrey Poitras, Department of Economics and Statistics, National University of Singapore

population. It is a gambling addict's chimera.

Of the figures mentioned in this chapter, two are worth saying a little more about, De Moivre and Petty.

Sir William Petty

William Petty was wholly created by the Sarpi networks around Francis Bacon and the Mersenne Circle. Throughout the entirety of his career, Petty was supported by the Cavendish family. This included financial backing from William Cavendish, the First Duke of Newcastle, the same individual who helped to organize the Mersenne network in Paris, and political/scientific backing by William's brother, the mathematician Charles Cavendish.

Petty knew many members of the Mersenne circle personally, but his closest relation was with Thomas Hobbes. Through the Cavendish family, Petty also became a rabid supporter of Francis Bacon and became a founding member of the "Invisible College," composed of Bacon's acolytes. His works abound with praise for Bacon, particularly in the preface to his *Anatomy of Ireland.* Not surprisingly Petty was also an enthusiastic champion of free markets and usury.

Abraham de Moivre, a Huguenot immigrant to England, was another project of the Cavendish family. After arriving in England, he was befriended by the William of Cavendish who was a leader of the 1688 plot to organize the takeover of England by William of Orange. Cavendish provided De Moivre with employment and introduced him to Isaac

Newton. In 1697, through the sponsorship of Newton and Edmund Halley, De Moivre became a member of the British Royal Society. In 1712 both De Moivre and Halley would play despicable roles in the rigged Royal Society proceedings, which lyingly upheld Newton's plagiarism charges against Leibniz on the authorship of the calculus.

De Moivre's writings, particularly the 1756 revised edition of *The Doctrine of Chances*, were very influential, and were later extensively discussed and referenced by a new generation of Sarpi's descendants, including Euler, Laplace, and others.

IX.   The Anglo-Dutch Empire

Death of Warwick - from Shakespeare's Henry VI

"If the circumstances stand so with your Highness that you believe you can get here time enough, in a condition to give assistances this year sufficient for a relief under these circumstances which have been now represented, we who subscribe this will not fail to attend your Highness upon your landing and to do all that lies in our power to prepare others to be in as much readiness as such an action is capable of..."
The *Letter of Invitation* to William of Orange, a secret message sent by Venice's fifth column in England, urging William III of the Netherlands, to launch his invasion of England.

Preparations for a Dutch invasion were underway throughout the spring and summer of 1688. Covert communications were maintained from the Orange Court at The Hague with the English conspirators, with Henry Sidney, the grand-nephew of Philip Sidney and the brother of Algernon, acting as the go-between. In England, Sidney's allies included William Cavendish, Lord Orford (Edward Russell), Lord Sunderland, and Bishop Compton, all pro-Dutch, and all in the Venetian orbit. After William of Orange landed in England, others rallied to the side of the Dutch, including Churchill (Marlborough), Portland, and Halifax. Contrary to some mistaken beliefs, this was not a peaceful walk-in-the-park "glorious revolution." It was an invasion. When William sailed for England, the Dutch invasion fleet consisted of 21,000

Earl of Shaftesbury

troops, massive artillery, and 500 ships. This force was four times larger than the famous invasion fleet of the Spanish Armada, a century earlier. On December 18, 1688, Dutch troops, under William's command, occupied London.

The pro-Empire grouping of English aristocrats who had organized the Dutch invasion became known as the Whig Junto, and they would be the new leadership of the nation. They publicly proclaimed a new motto for their regime—"Liberty & Property,"[57] and after 1688, crimes against property rose to great importance, with many being punishable by death. Under the new Whig regime, England developed the bloodiest penal code in all of Europe.

Many of these Whig leaders were proteges of Anthony Ashley Cooper (the 1st Earl of Shaftesbury). The arch-conspirator Cooper had served under several governments, including Cromwell and the Stuarts, but by the late-1660s, as the leader of the anti-Stuart CABAL (a forerunner of the Whig Junto), he was at the center of the Empire faction in Britain. He was the employer of John Locke, and in 1669, Locke authored the pro-slavery Constitution of Carolina for Shaftesbury. In 1681 Cooper fled to the Netherlands after

---

[57] This motto, which would later be paraphrased as "Life, Liberty, and Property" in the Constitution of the 1861-1865 Southern Confederacy, is to be contrasted with the Leibnizian commonwealth idea of "Life, Liberty, and the pursuit of Happiness."

he was charged with treason for plotting to overthrow the Stuarts. From the Netherlands, he helped organize, before his death, the 1684 Monmouth Plot, a failed plan for an invasion of England, to be launched from the Netherlands.

After 1688, the new institutions of Empire were rapidly put into place in London.[58] Venetian agents such as John Locke, Charles Montagu, and Isaac Newton, among others, were key to the London revolution in financial and monetary affairs.

In 1690, Locke's *Two Treatises on Government* was published, to provide the "philosophical" lattice for the transformation. In 1694 the Bank of England was founded. The next year saw Isaac Newton's "Great Recoinage," carried out under Locke's direction. In 1696 the Board of Trade and Plantations was established, with John Locke appointed as its first Commissioner of Trade,[59] and in 1698 the New East India Company was created. Within ten years of the Dutch invasion, the new institutions of Empire were all in place.

Clearing up misconceptions

Most historians misinterpret almost all of the events described above, because they view the struggle in England as one between the "democratic" Parliamentary forces of the Whigs versus the degenerate "divine right" Stuart monarchy, or, alternatively, between the Protestants and the Catholics. This is bad history. In truth, the conflict in England had deeper roots.

---

[58] The best source for the events which took place in England in these years is H. Graham Lowry's *How the Nation Was Won*.

[59] In the 18th century the Board of Trade became the political base for Lord Shelburne's (William Fitzmaurice Petty) operations against the American Revolution.

In the late 15th century, in the wake of the Council of Florence and the reign of Louis XI in France, a fight was waged in England, to overthrow the feudal dictatorship of Venice's Norman (Plantagenet) nobility, and to erect a sovereign nation-state. Henry Tudor's defeat of Richard III ushered in a new era of Erasmus, Thomas More, and John Colet, all conscious advocates of the Commonwealth idea. These developments were what Venice was determined to stop. After the death of Henry VII in 1509, and continuing throughout the entirety of the 16th century, the political situation in England was an ongoing battleground. But the real battle was not between Catholics and Protestants; it was between the Venetian-allied Empire faction on the one side, and the supporters of sovereignty and commonwealth on the other.

This battle was the underlying theme in all of the dramas of William Shakespeare, particularly in the portrait he paints of Venice's degenerate Plantagenet families in his "History" plays. In the 1520s, Henry VIII was corrupted by the Venetian agent Francesco Zorzi, and manipulated into the destruction of his own father's policies. Under Henry's daughter, Elizabeth I, the British Crown can only be described as under siege by Venice's English agents, including the Walsingham and Cecil families. During this period, several Venetian-style maritime trading companies were established, beginning with the Venice (sic) Company in 1586. This company went through several transitions and mergers and finally emerged in 1600 as the (old) East India Company. Eight years later the New Exchange, London's imitation of the Amsterdam Bourse was opened.

In 1603, with Venice's support,[60] James I of Scotland was installed as the new King, and his first Privy Council

---

[60] This included the role of Paolo Sarpi's ally Edwin Sandys, who was sent to Scotland to personally escort James I into London

included two men, Edward Wotton[61] and Robert Cecil, who personally were on intimate terms with Sarpi's *Giovani* leadership in Venice. This Venetian faction was the enemy which Shakespeare was organizing against during those years.

During the remainder of the 17th century, from the standpoint of the Empire, the question for England was what form was the new British oligarchical state to take. There were the Stuarts, there was Cromwell's regime (during which the power of the Empire crowd, as exemplified by the East India Company, continued to grow), and there were other potentialities.

By 1688, however, the corrupt and idiotic Stuarts where clearly past their use. Efforts were underway to transform England in the image of Amsterdam, and the Stuarts were in the way. One example of this is the Royal opposition to the creation of a Venetian-style Central Bank in London. Throughout the 17th century, oligarchical demands for the founding of such a bank grew into a chorus. The first I know of is the proposal, in 1646, by Benbrigge, for the creation of "a bank in the city of London as is at Amsterdam." Another similar proposal was made to Cromwell in 1657 by Samuel Lambe. In 1662, William Petty, in his *Treatise of Taxes and Contributions*, repeated these arguments. And, in 1676, Robert Murray published *A proposal for a National Bank*, calling for the establishment of a "Lombard Bank, modeled on the Bank of Amsterdam, incomparably the best bank in the world." There were many more, similar, proposals, some referencing the Bank of Amsterdam, others the Bank of Venice, and some both. After 1688 they would all get their wish.

---

[61] The brother of the English Ambassador and Sarpi agent Henry Wotton

The Bank of England

What historians call the British "financial revolution" of 1694-1698, was nothing less than a seizure of power within Britain by private oligarchical interests, and the diminution, and eventual subservience of the institutions of government to that oligarchy. There was a saying in the mid-18th century that the three pillars of British rule were "the Bank, the East India Company, and the Exchequer." Two of those three pillars were in private hands, beyond the reach of sovereign control, and the Exchequer (together with the Treasury) was effectively a fifth column of the oligarchy within the state institutions.

Moreover, what transpired in London, after 1688, was not a domestic revolution at all, but a foreign takeover, ostensibly by the Dutch, but actually by the Dutch-Venetian system of Empire. The founder of the Bank of England was William Paterson. He had been in Holland with William III, and active in effecting a Dutch invasion. The first Governor and the first Deputy Governor of the Bank were John Houblon and Michael Godfrey, both of whom had sat on the jury in 1681 which had acquitted the pro-Empire Lord Shaftesbury (Cooper) of high treason. The key agent of the Bank in the government was Charles Montagu (Lord Halifax), who had greeted William of Orange at the dock when his invasion fleet landed. Named Lord of the Treasury in 1692 and Lord of the Exchequer in 1694, it was Montagu who arranged the large government loans, which became the basis for the permanent national debt, a debt that would be controlled by the Bank. Later, in 1707, he became the British ambassador to Venice, but he returned once again to head the Treasury in 1714 after the takeover of the Hanoverian George I.

In terms of its character, the Bank of England went even

beyond the *Wisselbank* in its reach and power. One area where even the densest of historians have it right, is that the creation of the Bank of England was a defining moment in the emergence of modern private Central Banking. However, this is not due to many of the technical reasons that are usually given – even if those technicalities are important – but rather to the relationship between the Bank and the British state. In Amsterdam, the *Wisselbank*, the VOC, the Bourse, and the government all, more or less, coexisted. That may be a simplification, but for now, it is a useful simplification. In London, the financial oligarchy literally became the *de facto* government. The Parliament, the Privy Council, even the Church of England,[62] were absorbed into a Leviathan oligarchical entity, all of whose parts had a different function. Even to this day, there really

The original Bank of England

is no British "government" in any meaningful definition of that term which is legitimate. There is an oligarchy, a financial elite..... and an empire.

---

[62] This role of the Church as a pillar of oligarchical rule is associated with the English Arminians, and the Great Tew Circle.

In 1697, the first of a series of Acts was passed by Parliament, the end result being that the Bank was given a total monopoly over all banking in England. In 1707 the Bank took over the exclusive management of the national debt, which at that time, was £7 million, and growing. As the creditor of the national debt, that debt guaranteed the continued existence of the Bank. In 1742 the Bank was given the sole authority to issue bank notes, and its notes became the only legal tender (legal money) in all of Britain.

You have to grasp what you're looking at here. This is not the "normal functioning" of an economy. This is the Anglo-Dutch system. This is the beginning of European Central Banking. This is the deliberate handing over of sovereign economic, credit, and banking power to a private oligarchy.

The British East India Company

The original (old) East Company was founded in 1601, as one of several joint-stock companies (e.g., Virginia Company, Muscovy Company) to emerge in that period. In 1657, Oliver Cromwell issued a new charter for the Company which drastically changed its character, transforming it from a loosely knit group of merchants, into a centralized corporation with a permanent capital of £370,000. This change catalyzed a major expansion of East India Company operations in Asia between 1660 and 1690. This expansion was spearheaded by Sir Josiah Child, who from 1677 to 1690 was either Governor or Deputy Governor of the Company every year. Earlier, in 1668 Child had authored *A New Discourse of Trade*, which called for the use of Dutch financial and monetary methods in England.

After 1688, the entire nature of the Company was changed. No longer merely a large mercantile (albeit oligarchical) trading corporation, it was remade into a ruling pillar of the new British Empire.

In 1698, the "old" East India Company was dissolved and merged into the New East India Company. In 1708, under an agreement sponsored by Sydney Godolphin (an enemy of Jonathan Swift's), the power of the Company was vastly enhanced. It not only was granted extensive trading "privileges," it also became a direct partner with the Bank of England in controlling the finances of the British government, beginning with a £3.2 million loan to the government from the Company itself.

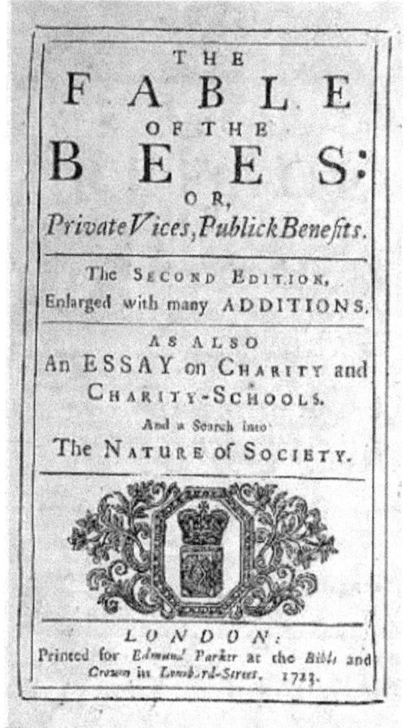

As was the case earlier with the Dutch VOC, the East India Company recruited its own army, built its own navy, waged its own wars, and collected all the loot. When the Company's army defeated the French at Plassey in 1757, all of India – hundreds of millions of people – came under the rule of the Company. India was not a British government or Crown colony. It was the property of the Company. They owned it. The Company coined its own money, which was legal tender in its dominions. And with the total defeat of the French in the Seven Years War, it was the Company, in 1763, which took possession of the French colonies and established a world-wide private empire.

The Final Nail in the Coffin

After the death of William III, a final battle was waged by England's patriots to prevent the subjugation of their nation. This fight was led by Jonathan Swift during the reign of Queen Anne.[63] In 1710, Swift's faction, including Robert Harley, Henry St. John (Bolingbroke), Matthew Prior, and the Duke of Ormond, took control of the British government. In 1711 they founded the South Sea Company as a rival to the Bank of England, and between 1711 and 1713, £9.4 million of government debt were exchanged for South Sea stock, eliminating the floating debt and cutting deeply into the power of the Bank. Swift and Harley's objective was to break the power of the Bank completely. The Empire counterattacked, and Amsterdam bankers organized a massive capital flight out of London, in an attempt to destroy Harley's government. After the death of Anne in 1714, Harley and Prior were both arrested and Bolingbroke and Ormond both fled to France, charged with treason.

Towards the end of his life, Bolingbroke described very clearly the enemy that Swift's faction was fighting in 1710: "The method of funding and the trade of stock-jobbing began. Thus were the *great companies* created, the pretended servants, but in many respects the *real masters* of every administration."

With the death of Queen Anne, Swift's faction was crushed, and the Empire crowd used the "Act of Settlement" to bring in George I of Hanover as the new British king. This triumph of the Empire was immediately celebrated with the London publication of Bernard Mandeville's paean to oligarchical culture, *The Fable of the Bees: or, Private Vices,*

---

[63] I provide here only a sketch of these events. See Lowry's *How the Nation Was Won* for the whole story.

Public Benefits. The following year Venetian master-spy and manipulator Antonio Conti arrived in England, and a new oligarchical puppet, Robert Walpole, was installed in 1721 as the head of the Treasury.

Within six months of George I's coronation, the Bank of England took over from the Exchequer the management of all government borrowing operations, and by 1719 the Bank was controlling most government stocks. The manipulation of those stocks, combined with loans by the Bank to the government, then became the means by which the Empire could carry out its global wars of expansion. This modus operandi was the key to financing all of the British wars of the 18th century, particularly the wars against France.

In 1742, Parliament not only gave the Bank the sole authority to print (fiat) money, it also said, "to prevent any doubt that may arise concerning the privilege or power given to the Bank of England of EXCLUSIVE BANKING... it is hereby further enacted and declared by the authority aforesaid, that it is the true intent and meaning of the said ACT, that no other bank shall be created, established or allowed by Parliament." For the next 80 years the Bank of England was the only joint-stock bank company allowed to exist in England.

Rule Britannia

The new London-based Empire was, of course, a maritime empire, and this would determine the geopolitical outlook of the Empire for the next two hundred years. It was an empire based on colonies, which were systematically looted of raw materials, agricultural products, and labor. At the same time, since the Empire's economic looting and military enforcement capabilities rested in the power of its fleet, no effort was spared to prevent the emergence of land-based economic powers, particularly across Eurasia.

A romantic mythology was created to portray Glorious England as the courageous island kingdom defending civilization. The romantic part is ludicrous claptrap, but there is a serious side to the mythology as well. As early as the reign of Elizabeth this theme of England as the great new maritime power was being discussed in various works of fiction and non-fiction. Scipio Gentili, with his long poem *Nereus*, Francis Bacon in the *New Atlantis*, and James Harrington in *Oceana*, all developed this theme in different ways. Harrington, who had spent years in Venice and who was a close friend of William Petty, believed that political power stems from economic riches, and *Oceana* describes an oligarchical society organized according to wealth.

Perhaps the most explicit writing in this vein was Nicholas Barbon's *A Discourse of Trade*. Published just two years after the Glorious Revolution, Barbon's work is a rabid hymn to free trade, supply and demand, and open-market economics. Concerning the establishment of Britain as a maritime empire, Barbon says,

"Those things that obstruct the growth of empire at land, do rather promote its growth at sea... The seat of such an empire must be an island, that their defense may be solely in shipping... England seems to be the proper seat for such an empire. It is an island, therefore requires no military force to defend it...The ships, excise and customs will in proportion increase, which may be so great in a short time, not only to preserve its ancient sovereignty over the narrow sea, but to extend its dominion over all the great ocean, an empire, not less glorious, and of a much larger extent, than either

Alexander's or Caesar's."[64]

Much later, in Queen Victoria's England, the British gadfly Walter Bagehot made the point of the advantage of London over Amsterdam as the seat of Empire. Writing in his 1873 ode to London finance, *Lombard Street*, Bagehot says, "The goodness of bank-notes depends on the solvency of the banker, and that solvency may be impaired if an invasion is not repelled, or a revolution resisted. Hardly any continental country has been till now exempt for long periods both from invasion and revolution. In Holland... there was never any security from foreign war."

Between 1689 and 1763 Britain and France fought four wars, lasting a total of 29 years. These were global conflicts. At the conclusion of the War of Spanish Succession in 1713, Britain was given the *asiento*, a monopoly over the importation of African slaves into Spain's Ibero-American colonies. They would hold this monopoly in the African slave trade for most of 18th century. The fourth English-French war (The Seven Years War) ended with the overwhelming defeat of France, the annihilation of the French navy, the bankruptcy of the French state, and the loss of the French colonies in India and North America. The Empire project was seemingly complete. The new London-based Empire was triumphant, and pre-eminent in power among all nations of the earth.

---

[64] In this same work Barbon makes an impassioned call for the creation of a Venetian-style public bank: "In Cities of great Trade, there are public Banks of Credit, as at Amsterdam and Venice; Public Banks are of so great a Concern in Trade, that the Merchants of London, for want of such a Bank, have been forced to Carry their Cash to Goldsmiths."

The Anglo-Dutch Axis

Much of what is written just above is well known. The error made by most historians is when they portray these events as a scenario of "dueling empires," i.e., "the British Empire versus the French Empire versus the Spanish Empire," etc. That fallacy misses the point that what was created from 1688 to 1763, was a *new type of empire*, fundamentally different from what had come before. Think of the British East India Company. Theirs was not an empire of the British nation, nor was it an empire of a monarch. It was an empire built for the benefit of a private financial oligarchy *which existed outside of and above the institutions of state.* Remember Locke's argument: private property is derived from the Law of Nature. Governments are created by men merely to safeguard that prior and superior right. 1688-1763 represented a maturation of the process that began in Venice, traveled through Amsterdam, and into London. And, of course, the Empire which emerged in London was not British; it was Anglo-Dutch.

1688 was not a transfer of the Empire's capital from Amsterdam to London; it was a takeover of England, a cloning of the Amsterdam financial institutions onto London, and a fusion of the financial and military capabilities of both nations to effect the creation of a power on behalf of Empire, greater than anything seen up to that time.

Initially, after 1688, the Netherlands was, by far, the greater of the two nations, both commercially and financially. In 1690, e.g., the VOC had 20,000 men is Asia, and the British East India Company only 1,000. Moreover, it was the financial resources of the Bank of Amsterdam and the Dutch money markets which created the Bank of England, and sustained it well into the 18th century. After

1690, and particularly after 1720, huge quantities of Dutch capital entered the English financial markets. By the 1730s, 30 percent of East India Company stock and 35 percent of Bank of England stock was held by the Dutch. Another ten percent of both companies was held by Geneva-based Swiss investors. By 1750 Dutch investors held 20 percent of the shares on the London Stock Exchange and held 26 percent of the England's national debt.

It was Amsterdam that remained the dominant financial power in Europe well into the 18th century. Even after the 1713 Treaty of Utrecht had established English maritime and commercial supremacy, *Amsterdam's financial power remained greater than London* up until the Napoleonic invasion of the Netherlands. The original capital of the Bank of England was £1.2 million. This was increased to 2.2 million in 1697 and 5.5 million in 1710; but this was a tiny fraction of the resources of the *Wisselbank*.

`The important point, however, is not to compare the relative power of London versus that of Amsterdam, but to look at how, as the 18th century progressed, the financial oligarchies of the two cities created a *unified Dutch/English financial monstrosity*.[65] The key to the integration of the London and Amsterdam markets was the trading in the stocks of the 5 big companies – the Dutch East India Company, the Dutch West India Company, the British East India Company, the Bank of England, and the South Sea Company. By no later than 1723, the two markets were tightly integrated. The two exchanges, in Amsterdam and London, functioned together, with daily shipments of financial contracts transported by ship between the two cities. Amsterdam speculators could take positions in the London exchange through corresponding attorneys, and

---

[65] *Efficient Markets in the Eighteenth Century? Stock Exchanges in Amsterdam and London,* by Larry Neal, University of Illinois at Urbana-Champaign

vice-versa. There was a certain division of labor between the two, and not surprisingly, it was Amsterdam that was the center of futures and options trading for all five companies. By the 18th century, the marketing of British Government and Bank of England bonds to Dutch speculators was indispensable to the financing of Britain's wars.[66] Between 1723 and 1794, neither country attempted an independent monetary policy. It was one operation.

---

[66] "Richard Cantillon, Financier to Amsterdam, July to November 1720," by Richard Hyse, *The Economic Journal*, Vol. 81, No. 324

Richard Cantillon – a case study

The life of Richard Cantillon is almost a microcosm of the Empire networks active in London, Amsterdam, and Paris during this period. Cantillon is most famous for his book *Essai Sur la Nature du Commerce en General* (Essay on the Nature of Commerce in General), originally published in Paris, in 1732. Adam Smith quotes Cantillon extensively in the Wealth of Nations, saying that Cantillon's book had a major influence on the French Physiocrats. Cantillon presents a strictly hedonistic market-driven theory of value, praises the Amsterdam Wisselbank to the skies, and anticipates Malthus, by writing, "Men multiply like mice in a barn if they have the means of subsistence without limit." Today, free-market "economists" of the Austrian School have high praise for Cantillon, considering him sort of a John Law, "without the flaws."

In Paris, Cantillon was an ally of the speculator John Law, and he reportedly made more than 20 million livres from speculating in the stock of Law's Mississippi Company. Cantillon got out of the French market before the crash, with all of his money.

Having participated in the financial ruin of the French nation, Cantillon moved to Amsterdam in 1720, and spent the rest of his life traveling back and forth between London and Amsterdam. He established an insurance company and spent years as a major financial speculator. While in Amsterdam, Cantillon played an important role in organizing the bear raid against the South Sea Company stock, which was used to politically finish off the last of the patriotic networks associated with Jonathan Swift in England.

X. The Nature of the Beast

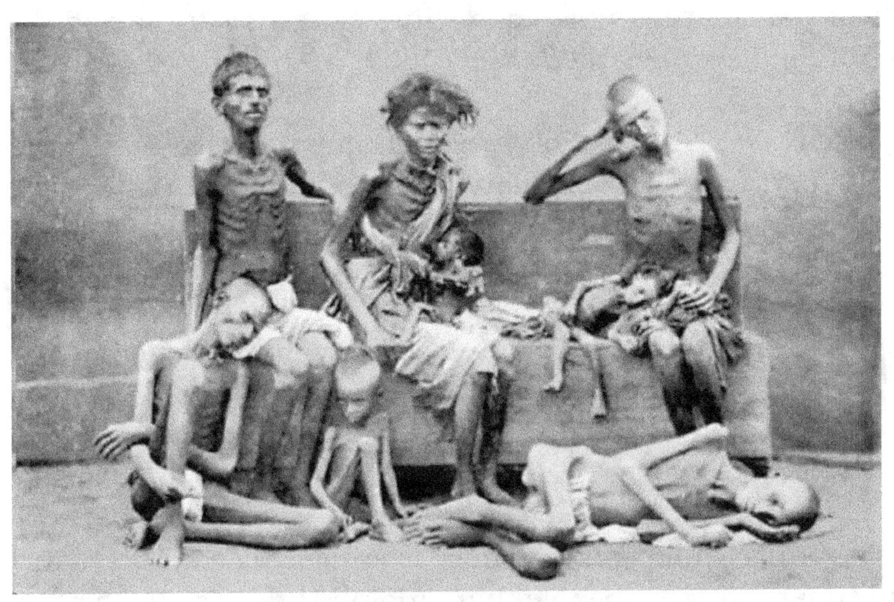

An Indian Family during the 1876 famine

Question: "What was the nature of the London-based creature which came into existence at the end of the Seven Years War in 1763?"

Answer: "A global oligarchical Empire based on usury, financial speculation, slavery, drug-trafficking, private central banking, and permanent war."

Discussing the British Empire with people today is a fascinating experience. When the issue of that Empire's crimes against humanity comes up, not untypical responses are either denial, disbelief, or a desire to change the subject. The fact that the British Empire was the world's leading slave trader, leading drug trafficker, and killed far, far more people than Adolph Hitler, is all a matter of irrefutable public record. It was all done *out in the open*, over a period of more than two centuries. The fact that that same Empire is based on axiomatic principles hostile to the American Republic, and has been the mortal enemy of the United States down to the present day, may be a little more difficult for people to see, but not that much more difficult. The problem is not a lack of evidence; it is simply an hysterical unwillingness to just face the facts.

This seeming inability to accept the provable charges against the British Empire is a perfect example of the success of the oligarchy in getting many people to believe – in the words of Bertrand Russell – that "snow is black."

However, even if 99 percent of the population is willing to swear under oath that "snow is black," or at least grey, that doesn't alter the truth that snow is white.

Consider this: In recent years there has been a demand, put forward by some, that the United States government apologize for slavery. Have the British ever apologized for being the leading slave trader in the world for almost two centuries?   Recently, the Roman Catholic Church apologized for its history of anti-Semitism. Have the British ever apologized about their history of racist colonialism, about the millions they killed in India, about their forced addiction of tens of millions in China to narcotics? Have the British ever formally or informally apologized for any of their crimes? Far from it. They're proud of their record. In their view, Britain's history has been an almost heroic saga of spreading civilization to the rest of humanity. Try selling that crap to their victims.

Then there is the claim that all of these crimes are a thing of the past, that the Empire is merely a memory. The answer to that charge is simply, "You're still calling snow black." The truth is that after 1945 the British (and the Dutch) did everything in their power to hang onto their colonies, *until they were forced to give most of them up* over a period of years that culminated in the Presidency of John F. Kennedy. However, that was not the end of the Empire. Beginning in the years immediately after World War II, and then escalating dramatically after 1971, London has been engaged in creating a new form of colonialism, under the guise of "globalization," – utilizing banks not bullets – which is actually far more pernicious and murderous than their previous methods.

For now, let's look at the charges leveled against the Anglo-Dutch Empire in the above Q & A...

Slavery

Slavery pre-dates the modern Anglo-Dutch Empire, but it does not pre-date Empire. It is the very essence of Empire. The relegation of the vast majority of the human race to the category of "sub-human property" is at the heart of the Olympian oligarchical world-view. The imperial use of slavery goes back, at least, to the days of Babylon. It is defended openly in the writings of Aristotle. All of Roman Law is explicit on the property rights of slave owners, and the Roman empire was built and maintained on slave labor.[67]

By the 12th and 13th centuries, the slave trade was one of the biggest businesses in the Mediterranean, and the dominant player was the Venetian Empire. Venice was the slave market of the world. In the years following the Council of Florence, the first systematic legal defense of slavery is to be found in the writings of the Salamancans, whose job was to justify the massive expansion of slavery by the Spanish Empire. Later, those arguments would be repeated by Grotius and John Locke in their defenses of the practices of the Dutch and British Empires.

At the same time, the economic subjugation of populations defines the essence of human slavery just as much as the legal institution of chattel slavery itself. After the collapse of Rome, the feudal system of Diocletian condemned the population of medieval Europe to an hereditary bondage, perhaps even worse than legal slavery. In the 19th century, the American patriot Henry Carey dissected the colonial economic policies of the British in Ireland and India, and proved conclusively that this was *de*

---

[67] Many of the Roman Law arguments defending slavery were copied directly by Di Vitoria, Grotius, Locke, et al.

facto, if not *de jure*, the slavery of tens of millions.[68]

The institution of slavery is not something that existed at one "stage" of man's history, a "stage" we have now outgrown. It does not represent a part of human culture that we have now recognized as evil. *It was never part of real human culture, of the culture that made human progress possible. It is a principle of Empire. The degradation of large numbers of people to legal or de facto slavery is a necessary practice of Empire. Slavery is, in fact, probably the most basic axiom of the Empire outlook.*

Consider the following:

The Spanish, Portuguese, Dutch and British empires were all built and maintained by slave labor. Only 11 years after Christopher Columbus' first voyage, a Spanish royal decree legalized the slave trade and the importation of slaves into the new world. Between 1500 and 1650, Spain and Portugal dominated the slave traffic. Initially, most of the slaves went to the gold and silver mines of Mexico and South America, but, by 1600, the vast majority were going to the sugar, indigo, tobacco, and rice plantations of Brazil and the Caribbean.

The first official Dutch slave ship sailed in 1606, five years after the founding of the VOC. In 1621 the Dutch West India Company was founded, with its main purpose being to challenge Spain and Portugal's control over the African slave trade. This was accomplished by mid-century, as the Dutch seized most of the Spanish and Portuguese slave fortresses in West Africa.[69] The Dutch were also given the *Asiento de Negros* by the Spanish Crown. This was a

---

[68] *The Slave Trade, Domestic and Foreign: Why it Exists, and How it May Be Extinguished*, by Henry C. Carey, 1853

[69] There were 42 slave fortresses in western Africa, the most important of which was Elmina (Sao Jorge da Mina). It was built by the Portuguese in 1481, and held by them until the Dutch captured it in 1637. By the 18th century, 30,000 slaves per year passed through Elmina on route to the Americas.

legal monopoly over the right to import slaves into Spain's colonies, which were, by far, the biggest market for slaves in the world. The Dutch would hold the *Asiento* until 1713, when it was given to the British at the Treaty of Utrecht. By 1676 the Dutch were selling 15,000 slaves per year in the Americas.

The vast Dutch Empire in Asia was also based on slavery. The Dutch East India Company took slaves by the tens of thousands from East Africa, Madagascar, New Guinea, the Philippines, Malaysia, and Indonesia. By 1700,

The Portuguese-Dutch Elmina slave fortress in west Africa

the population of the VOC capital at Batavia was 52 percent slaves. In Capetown it was 42 percent, Colombo - 53 percent, and Makassar - 66 percent. A global empire... built on slavery.

After 1713, the new London-based Empire would next demonstrate what amateurs their predecessors had been. According to most sources, 70 percent of all the slaves taken from Africa between 1500 and 1850, were shipped between

1700 and 1800. This was the pinnacle of the global slave system. It was also the period when the British had a near monopoly on the trade. The record was set in 1768, when a staggering 110,000 human beings were taken from Africa and sold into slavery. And of course it was the British who brought slavery into their North American colonies. Under Paolo Sarpi's friend Edwin Sandys, the Virginia Company brought the first slaves into Jamestown in 1618, and the first public slave auction was conducted in 1638. By 1715, twenty-four percent of Virginia's population were slaves.

What is little know today, is that between 1680 and 1776, the massive importation of slaves by the British Empire into the American colonies was carried out – by royal decree – *against fierce opposition by the colonists*, who did not want a slave-based economic system.[70]

Between 1450 and 1850 at least 20 million Africans were either taken as slaves, or killed as a result of the slave trade. According to the historian W.E.B. Du Bois, between 1600 and 1800, about 12 million slaves were brought into the Americas, totaling about 60 percent (i.e. a majority) of all trans-Atlantic emigration. This is the legacy of Empire. This is what British aristocrats call the benevolent "spreading of civilization."

Genocide & War

From the 17th through the 19th century, there were many, many wars fought among the European powers, but, for our present purpose, it is more useful to look at the so-called colonial wars waged throughout that period, because those wars both define something essential about the nature of Empire, and they are also the model for the

---

[70] *Race is not the Issue!*, by Robert Ingraham, *Executive Intelligence Review*, Aug. 25, 2017

financial oligarchy's plans for the 21st century. Beginning with the Operation Desert Storm of Margaret Thatcher and President George Bush, we have now entered the era of rapid-deployment-force types of regional and "limited" wars, designed to crush all opposition to the economic looting of globalization. As former Vice President Dick Cheney had made clear, – and as was continued under eight years of the Obama Presidency – in discussing the "War on Terror," this is designed to be an open-ended regime of permanent global warfare. Empires may fight big wars if they have no choice, but it is the policy of continuous permanent war against targeted populations which is the basis for the looting, enforced backwardness, and subjugation of people all over the world.

Beginning with the attempt by the British to crush the American colonists in 1775, and continuing well into the 20th century, the British Empire engaged in what can only be called *permanent colonial war*. As one historian has described it:

> "There was not a single year in Queen Victoria's long reign in which somewhere in the world her soldiers were not fighting for her and her empire. From 1837 until 1901, in Asia, Africa, Arabia, and elsewhere, British troops were engaged in almost constant combat."[71]

A few of the more notable examples of the carnage unleashed by the British, include the Sikh Wars in India from 1845 to 1850, the Flagstaff War and related campaigns, which lasted for decades in New Zealand, the 1879 Zulu War in Africa, the 1856 Anglo-Persian War, the

---

[71] *Queen Victoria's Little Wars,* by Byron Farwell, W.W. Norton and Co., New York, 1985

1854-55 Crimean War, the Boer Wars, beginning in 1880, and the Indian Sepoy Rebellion in 1857, at the conclusion of which tens of thousands of Indians were butchered in cold blood.

These are only a few examples, and they don't even begin to tell the story of the genocide perpetrated by the British Empire. It is also crucial to grasp that the tens (or hundreds) of thousands killed in the Empire's military campaigns were a tiny fraction of the total victims of the economic rape imposed by the Empire on its victims.

British mass murder in India was so horrific and blatant, that even at the time it was perpetrated, members of the British Parliament denounced the crimes of their nation. Henry Carey quotes the words of British Parliamentarian George Thompson, who described these scenes during the 1838 famine in British India:

"Go with me into the north-western provinces of the Bengal presidency, and I will show you the bleaching skeletons of five hundred thousand human beings, who perished of hunger in the space of a few short months. Yes, died of hunger... The air for miles was poisoned by the effluvia emitted from the putrefying bodies of the dead. The rivers were choked with the corpses thrown into their channels... Jackals and vultures approached, and fastened upon the bodies of men, women, and children, before life was extinct. Madness, disease, despair stalked abroad, and no human power present to arrest their progress. It was the carnival of death! And this occurred in British India—in the reign of Victoria the First! Nor was the event extraordinary and unforeseen. Far from it: 1835-36 witnessed a famine in the northern provinces; 1833 beheld one to the eastward; 1822-23 saw one in the Deccan. They have continued to increase in frequency and extent under our sway for more than half a century."

Carey goes on to show, that far from an act of God, the famines and mass starvation in India were the direct and intended effect of the British economic policies which had destroyed the native economy and agriculture of India.[72] He also documents how, at the height of the 1838 famine, the British were exporting more than 151 million pounds of rice out of India, as a cash crop, in order to pay foreign debts and taxes. This, of course, is the same thing that the World Trade Organization is telling the nations of Africa, Asia, and South America to do today. After detailing the total subjugation and impoverishment of the Indian people, Carey concludes, "This is slavery, and under such a system how could the wretched people be other than slaves?"

It is estimated that the Indian famines between 1822 and 1838 killed as many as 29 million people.[73] Adolph Hitler took 12 years to kill 6 million Jews. In 16 years the British managed to kill five times that number. And it didn't stop in 1838. During the famine in the Deccan plateau region, in 1876, there was a surplus of rice and wheat in India. But the British Viceroy insisted that nothing should prevent its export to England. At the height of the famine, a record 320,000 tons of wheat were exported, while hundreds of thousands of Indians died.

The genocide against the people of Ireland was almost identical in method to that in India. After centuries of British rule, more than 75 percent of the Irish were tenant farmers in 1845, i.e. they were the equivalent of feudal serfs and, in real terms, owned by their aristocratic Lords. They

---

[72] Carey, op. cit.
[73] *Late Victorian Holocausts,* by Mike Davis, Verso Books, 2001

were, in effect, slaves. They were the poorest people in Europe, whose normal condition was one step ahead of starvation. They ate no meat and very little of anything else. Meanwhile, almost all of the oats, corn, wheat, and barley grown in Ireland were exported as cash crops by British landlords, acting in collusion with London financiers. In addition to stealing Ireland's agricultural bounty, the British also extracted millions of pounds yearly in rents and taxes from the island.

In 1845 a potato blight wiped out three-quarters of the island's production of potatoes, the main staple in the diet of the destitute Irish, and a second, worse, blight hit the following year's crop as well. In 1846, as people were dying by the tens of thousands, British officials exported from Ireland enough wheat, barley, oats, butter, pigs, and eggs to feed the entire population, and those record levels of "cash crop" exports continued through 1847-1849, as hundreds of thousands starved to death. By the time it was all over, more than 2 million Irish were dead. In 1844 the population of Ireland was over 8 million. It is still lower than that today.

British rule in Ireland and India may rise to the level of Hitlerian crimes, but the experiences of those two nations is not unique. Literally millions were killed across the globe, especially in Africa. Consider this description of British activities in Kenya, in the 1950s, as they desperately tried to hold on to their colony:

"Thrown off their best land and deprived of political rights, the Kikuyu started to organize against colonial rule. The British responded by driving up to 320,000 of them into concentration camps. Most of the remainder — more than a million — were held in 'enclosed villages.' Prisoners were questioned with the help of 'slicing off ears, boring holes in eardrums, flogging until death, pouring paraffin over suspects who were then set alight, and burning eardrums with lit cigarettes.' The soldiers were told they could shoot anyone they liked 'provided they were black.' The evidence suggests that more than 100,000 Kikuyu were either killed or died of disease and starvation in the camps."[74]

Drugs

The story of the Britain's Opium Wars against China is well known. What is less well known, except by some experts, is the open British control of world narcotics traffic all the way up until World War II, and that, today, it is the unregulated financial institutions in British Crown colonies, such as the Cayman Islands, which continue to finance the bulk of international drug production and trafficking. Forty years ago the authors of *Dope, Inc.*[75] demonstrated that narcotics trafficking is the biggest business in the world, and that major financial institutions, like the Hong-Kong & Shanghai Bank, control the drug trade, through their control over the money. Narcotics trafficking, like slavery, is a necessary activity of the modern Anglo-Dutch Empire. That Empire has played the controlling role in global drug trafficking since its inception, and it continues to play that role today. On the one hand, it is a business which makes hundreds of billions of dollars. On the other hand, it is an indispensable method – as was seen in 19th century China, and as we have seen in the

---

[74] *Imperial Reckoning: the Untold Story of Britain's Gulag in Kenya*, by Caroline Elkins, Henry Holt Publishers, 2006

[75] *Dope, Inc. - Britain's Opium War Against the United States*, by Kalimtgis, Goldman, and Steinberg, New Benjamin Franklin House, New York, 1978

United States and Europe since 1963 – of destroying the moral and political capabilities of populations to resist Imperial rule.[76]

As soon as the British East India Company consolidated its rule over the Indian province of Bengal in 1757, they began turning whole sections of the countryside into opium plantations. This involved taking land out of food production, with the murderous results discussed above. The British were not the first to do this; the Dutch had begun even earlier, with the pacifying of the Indonesian population through mass opium addiction as early as 1659, but the British would go way beyond anything the Dutch had attempted. The first East India Company shipments of opium into China began in 1781, and the volume of the trafficking increased steadily into the second and third decades of the 19th century.

By the 1830s there were more than 10 million drug addicts in China, and when the Chinese government acted in 1838 to wipe out the drug trade, the British responded by going to war. They sent a fleet of 16 warships to China which bombarded the cities, killed tens of thousands, and threatened the Chinese capital. The Chinese government was forced to capitulate in 1842, but even then, facing the gunboats of the Empire, the Chinese Emperor refused to accept the British demand for the total legalization of opium trafficking. Not satisfied with these heinous actions, the British launched a second war against China in 1856, this time forcing the complete surrender of the Chinese government, and the formal legalization of all drug trafficking. By 1880 there were 40 million opium addicts in China, all supplied with opium produced by the British in India, brought into China by British ships, and financed by

---

[76] Consider the role of mega-speculator and London agent, George Soros, in financing multiple efforts for drug legalization in the United States

British banks.

How did the British defend these actions? Simple, they didn't. Their claim was that the wars against China had nothing to do with drugs(!!!), but that the *causus belli* of the war – which justified the English military onslaught – were the Chinese protectionist measures which were injurious to the British democratic policies of Free Trade—the exact same argument used by Francisco di Vitoria to justify Spain's extermination of the American Indians 300 years earlier. After the British Crown took over the governing of India from the East India Company and Queen Victoria was named the Empress of India in 1876, all of the narcotics going into China were trafficked under her personal authority.

In the early 20th century, against fierce British and Dutch opposition, the United States initiated legal and diplomatic efforts to halt opium (and by now heroin) trafficking. One of America's first acts after the Spanish-American War, was to outlaw opium production in the Philippines and shut down the drug plantations. Between 1909 and 1914, four international conferences were held, all at American insistence, aimed at curbing the drug trade. All failed due to British opposition. After the founding of the League of Nations in 1920, a renewed effort was undertaken to curtail the global trade in opium and heroin. Cooperation in this effort was almost universal except for the British Empire. In 1923, an American proposal was brought before the League of Nations to reduce worldwide opium production by 90 percent. It was killed by the British delegation. The League of Nations held two conferences in Geneva in 1925, with similar outcome.

During this period, the British were actually expanding their drug pushing. In 1927 official British government figures showed that in many of Britain's Asian colonies, including Malaysia, Borneo, and Sarawak, profits from the drug trade accounted for over 30-50 percent of the government's revenues. *In India, during the same period, Mahatma Gandhi was leading demonstrations against Britain's plans to expand opium production.* In 1931, the League of Nations held three more conferences aimed at increasing the restrictions and penalties for drug production and trafficking. The U.S. Government refused to sign the final agreement, because it did not go far enough and contained loopholes inserted by the British. Throughout this whole period, all the way up to the outbreak of war in 1939, the minutes of the Advisory Committee of the League's Opium Commission, document the British Crown's continued role in the trafficking and distribution of opium and heroin.

These drug-pushing activities of the British Empire were also mimicked by their Dutch partners. Between 1895 and 1904 the cultivation of opium in Indonesia by privately held farms was replaced by a policy known as the *regie system*, whereby the Dutch colonial government took effective control of all opium production.[77] During the next ten years opium production and consumption increased dramatically, and, under Dutch colonial control, new strains of opium were developed which increased the morphine content of the opium by up to 30 percent. This official Dutch drug production continued up until the Japanese invasion during World War II.

Narcotics trafficking is not merely a business. In fact, its primary purpose is not as a business at all. For more than three centuries, the overriding intent of the imperial British drug pushers has been to enslave and subjugate populations. Global drug trafficking was created by the

---

[77] *The Role of Government Policy in Increasing Drug Use: Java, 1875-1914,* by Siddharth Chandra

Dutch and British empires, and it is that same Anglo-Dutch financial empire which controls narcotics trafficking to this day. Furthermore, it is the agents of that Empire, such as George Soros, who continue to organize for an expansion of drug use and legalization.

Since the 1960s, several generations of American and European youth have been brainwashed into the idea of "recreational drug use" as a human right. This tragedy acutely demonstrates the intended success of the Empire in destroying the moral and mental strength of the younger generations. The heart-rending picture of first Baby Boomer, then Tweener, then Generation X and now Millennial youth demanding drug legalization is nothing less than an African native walking up to British slave-traders and begging to have the chains and shackles put on.

Look at the accompanying photograph of Richard Grasso, the President of the New York Stock Exchange embracing Raul Reyes of the narco-terrorist FARC, in the jungles of Colombia in 1999. Think of the lives destroyed by crack cocaine in cities across the United States, and consider what that photograph actually means. Consider also the role of the offshore banks and hedge

Grasso & Reyes: a picture worth 1,000 words

funds in the British Cayman Islands and the Dutch Antilles

in financing this evil. This is British Free Trade. This is globalization. This is the continuing modern face of Empire.

Central Banking

To return to a basic theme of this work, the 1582-1763 Venice-Amsterdam-London creation of modern private Central Banking was, in its nature, axiomatically, the opposite of the Renaissance concept of the Commonwealth. *These two different approaches to ordering human affairs are not only incompatible, they are eternal antagonists. The one is based on a supremacy of the fondi, the rich oligarchical interest, where governments are deployed as servants of private financial interests and money is "king." The other is built on a foundation of national sovereignty, and a commitment to the General Welfare of all of the people, including a commitment to the nation's posterity, through policies which foster scientific and technological progress.* What we today call "European Central Banking," derives from institutions created in Venice, Amsterdam and London, the birthplaces of the oligarchical financial model. How we went from those early beginnings to today's global System of Central Banking is the next part of the story.

This global oligarchical banking system was created almost exclusively in two locations—the European continent, and the colonies of the British Empire. The creation of this system took place in two stages, the first following the 1815 Treaty of Vienna, and the second after 1876, as the British Empire moved to stop the spread of American influence in Asia and continental Europe. Two of the major contributing factors which made these developments possible were the total subjugation of France after the Napoleonic Wars, and the creation of the British global Gold Standard.

The way to understand the British gold standard is to keep in the forefront of your mind the word "subjugation." Today, no one except denizens of the neo-con fringe would propose a return to a pre-1931 hard gold standard. What most people fail to realize, is that even in the 19th century, it was generally recognized by almost everyone that the gold standard was sheer lunacy from an economic standpoint. *It was not an economic policy; it was a geopolitical policy, intended to insure British domination.* Britain's control over world gold markets gave London enormous influence over foreign banks and governments. In the 1830s, for example, huge amounts of American securities were held in London, and many American banks were completely dependent on the Bank of England for financing. Britain blackmailed nations into joining the gold standard, and then imposed central banks on them to manage their balance of payments.

In the wake of the Napoleonic Wars, Great Britain forced a weakened Spain to hand over all of the Spanish gold and silver mines in South America. Then, in 1819, the British Parliament voted to adopt a strict monetary gold standard. This went into effect in 1821, and would last until 1931. This original gold standard was further extended and codified by the 1842 Bank Charter Act, which tied the issuance of all new currency to a one-to-one ratio of gold and silver on deposit. Any increase in bank-note issuance was tied directly to an increase in specie reserves, thus creating probably the most rigid deflationary gold standard in human history. Britain itself experienced great difficulty in managing this policy, even with her vast gold reserves. For other nations, the gold standard was an economic death sentence which made impossible any serious physical economic development.

With the domination of world trade and finance by the British Empire during the 19th century, London was able to blackmail, threaten, and bankrupt nations almost at will. Almost total British control over the Bank of France during this period served to augment their financial and monetary power. These were also the years when the British did everything in their power to destroy the emergence of National Banking and Hamiltonian Economics in the United States.[78]

The real threat to the Empire came in the years following the Union victory over the British-created Confederacy in the American Civil War. The industrial transformation of the United States, – resulting from Abraham Lincoln's Greenback and National Banking policies – together with the spread of American economic methods to Germany, Russia, Japan, and China, created a profound crisis for the maritime British Empire. Their response was to prepare the way for World War One, and the British elites were preparing for such a war by no later than 1894. Additionally, the British moved to counter the spread of American economic policies by creating a System of Central Banks under British control. Between 1876 and 1914, central banks, based explicitly on the British model, were established in Germany, Italy, Sweden, Switzerland, Austria, Belgium, Denmark, Japan, and other nations. In some cases there were intense battles in these nations over whether to adopt an American-style National Bank, or British private Central Banking. The British were in a war against the American system and, in the process, they were attempting to establish the Amsterdam-London model as the international banking paradigm. Lets take a look at what happened in some of these nations:

---

[78] *Treason in America,* by Anton Chaitkin

Germany – the German *Reichsbank* was founded 1875, and then given greater powers in the banking "reform" of 1909. The *Reichsbank* was wholly owned by private investors, yet it ran all the monetary functions of the government. From very early on the *Reichsbank* assumed the full role of a Central Bank, issuing notes, regulating the financial system, and clearing commercial paper.   In 1900 the Directors of Reichsbank published a pamphlet in which they stated "the most important and likewise the most difficult task of the bank is to bring about the greatest possible equalization of fluctuations in money demands and to be at all times in a position to redeem its notes and to meet its other liabilities." The two paramount priorities set by the bank were to maintain the gold standard and to foster the well-being of the financial system.

Switzerland – the *Swiss National Bank* was founded in 1905, modeled on the *Reichsbank*. Earlier, in 1891 a proposal had been debated to create a state-owned bank, with a monopoly on note issuance. This proposal was killed by opponents who wanted a completely private bank. The charter of the 1905 bank stated that "The National Bank has for its principal objects to regulate the money market of the country, and to facilitate payments and transfers of money," and also "The purpose of the Bank is to regulate the Swiss monetary system."

Sweden – the famous *Riksbank* claims to be one of the oldest Central Banks in the world, dating from 1668, but actually its modern charter was adopted in 1897, at which point it was recreated on the British model, and given a monopoly on the issuance of (gold-backed) notes.

Denmark – another older bank that was overhauled in this period was the Danish National Bank, which was given a new charter in 1908, which included all the features of a modern central bank.

Italy – possessed several regional "banks of issuance." However, in 1893 the *Banca d'Italia* was created, for the purpose of regulating and protecting the activities of the private local banks.

Austria – again a "reformed" older bank. Austria had been on the silver standard, but after the British-manipulated crash of 1873, they were forced to shift into gold. The *Austro-Hungarian Bank* was given a new charter, with most of the features of a private central bank, with its main responsibility being to maintain the gold exchange rate.

Belgium – following several financial crises in the 1830s, one of which forced the Bank of Belgium to suspend gold convertibility, a new *National Bank of Belgium* was founded in 1850. Like many of the other European banks, it too, in 1900, was given a new charter, with a monopoly on the issuance of currency and other Central Banking responsibilities.

Japan – Japan was a battleground. After the Meiji restoration in 1866, and through the influence of Henry Carey's ally, E. Peshine Smith, there was an attempt to establish a National Bank explicitly on the American model, but according to a report written by Baron Sakatani, the former Japanese Minister of Finance, "It was found, however that such a national bank system did not work well on account of its being unsuitable to national conditions, and the regulations were amended in 1876 and 1882, when the central bank system was adopted."

Actually the fledgling national banking system was sabotaged between 1866 and 1876 by repeated demands by bank note holders for specie redemption of their national bank notes. In 1883, a new private Central Bank, the *Bank of Japan* was given the monopoly over note issuance. In 1888 gold convertibility resumed, and in 1897 Japan officially joined the gold standard.

France – France has a long banking history, but the modern *Banque de France* was created in 1800, totally under the control of private shareholders. A revealing quote from a French banker in 1870 gives the thinking behind this bank: "The foreign enemy could not, because of the private character of the bank, consider its wealth as spoils of war, without trampling underfoot international law.[79] The case would have been entirely different had the Bank been a state bank. This is an advantage not to be neglected."

During the 19th century, the bank maintained an incestuous relationship with the large private banks, i.e., Rothschild, Davillier, Mallet, Hottinguer, etc. However, its primary role was as an asset of the Bank of England. Because of its large gold reserves (second in the world only to the Bank of England), the French bank was frequently tapped by the British for specie and other financial assistance. During several financial crises, including those of 1825, 1836-39, 1890, and 1906-07, the role of the *Banque de France* was crucial to Britain's ability to maintain the international gold standard.

---

[79] Since oligarchical "International Law" protects oligarchical private property rights, but not defeated sovereign nations (RDI)

During the 20th century the Central Banking System was extended further. First, after World War I, the British installed central banks in the new nations created by the Versailles Treaty, including Austria in 1923, Hungary in 1924, and Czechoslovakia in 1926. At the same time, either central banks, or subsidiaries of the Bank of England, were

The European Central Bank

established in British colonies, including the Bank of Adelaide, the Bank of New South Wales, the Queensland National Bank (all 3 in Australia), the Bank of New Zealand, the Imperial Bank of India, the Bank of Ireland, the Hong Kong and Shanghai Bank, and other banks in Scotland and Canada. In 1911 the Commonwealth Bank of Australia was established with limited Central Bank functions. In addition, other British-dominated banks were established in non-Empire countries, such as the *Banco do Brasil*, the *Bank Melli* (Iran), and the National Bank of Egypt.

Since 1971, this Central Banking monstrosity has gone much, much further in attempting to destroy all national economic sovereignty and to impose rule by a global elite. More will be said on this in the final chapter, but for now, just consider the fate of Europe. As of 2008, not only have the nations of Europe surrendered most of their political sovereignty, but even the Central Banks mentioned above, have become little more than appendages of the new *European Central Bank*, created in 1998 by virtue of the

Maastricht Treaty, This private bank, under the control of the Anglo-Dutch faction, is completely independent from any European national government or institution. *It answers to no government, yet it has the power to dictate monetary, budgetary and credit policies*, both to its individual member banks, as well as to all of the "nations" of the European Union. If the recently proposed Lisbon Treaty were to be adopted, it would extend those powers even further, to the point that national sovereignty in Europe would cease to exist altogether.

There are two final points to make on this subject. The first is to keep in mind that this global System of private Central Banking is a recent creation. Most of these institutions were established in a 55 year period from 1876 to 1931.[80] Empire may be the ancient enemy of humanity, but the global Central Banking System is not a centuries-old institution. It is also not an axiomatic pre-existing feature of human culture. It is a creation, and a very modern creation at that, whose existence is becoming more and more tenuous every day.

———

The final point to be made concerns the anti-human outlook or philosophy of this System. In his piece *The Truth About Temporal Eternity*,[81] Lyndon LaRouche demonstrates that the post-1763 oligarchical outlook of the British Empire, as expressed in the writings of Adam Smith and, later, Jeremy Bentham,[82] goes even beyond the

---

[80] In 1931, the power of the global Central Banking System was enhanced with the founding of the Swiss-based Bank of International Settlements

[81] "The Truth About Temporal Eternity," by Lyndon H. LaRouche Jr., *Fidelio*, Summer 1994 (Vol. III, No. 2)

[82] See Smith's *Theory of Moral Sentiments* and Bentham's *In Defense of Usury*

prescriptions of John Locke, or the earlier French, Dutch, and Scottish Calvinists. Many of the 17th century oligarchical "legal theorists," discussed above in Chapter 7, stressed custom and "common law" as a philosophical justification for oligarchical rule. LaRouche makes the point that with Adam Smith and his followers, all concerns for custom, or even human culture itself, vanishes. By the 19th century, an outright satanic empiricism is dominant. Money reigns supreme; avarice is the law of the land; and military force is deployed to defend this system.

The use of the term satanic is not an exaggeration. Beginning with Mandeville's *Fable of the Bees*, through the activities of the 18th century London Hell-Fire Clubs, and into the works of Jeremy Bentham and Adam Smith, the ideology of the British Empire was based on a totally bestial view of human nature—on the idea that the pursuit of hedonistic pleasure is both the axiomatic nature of the human species, as well as the driving force behind all human economic activity. Bentham defined this as his *hedonistic calculus*, and Bentham's utilitarian philosophy has defined the outlook of the British Empire down to the present day.

Consider the charters of the Central Banks discussed above, where they proclaim as priorities "to regulate the money market of the country, and to facilitate payments and transfers of money," and "to bring about the greatest possible equalization of fluctuations in money demands." This is a global system based on individual greed and the "supremacy of money," as if money somehow pre-dated human existence.

Now consider the following quote from the *Frame of the Government of Pennsylvania* (1682), written by William Penn: "When the great and wise God had made the world, of all his creatures, it pleased him to chuse man his Deputy to rule it: and to fit him for so great a charge and trust, he did not only qualify him with skill and power, but with integrity to use them justly..."

Where in the universe of central banking does such an idea have a place? The central bankers don't even recognize Penn's concept of Man as relevant. Adam Smith would have us all enslaved to our greed and passions, living like beasts in an atomistic universe. This is real naked evil, the denial of everything which is truly human, which you will see... if you are willing to open up your eyes and look at it.

XI. The American Commonwealth & Alexander Hamilton

Gottfried Leibniz

From the signing of the Mayflower Compact in 1620, through to the conclusion of the Constitutional Convention in 1787, the greatest triumph in the ordering of human affairs, in all of history, was accomplished. It was accomplished largely by Europeans, but Europeans who had come to these shores to create something which was no longer possible in Europe. As John Winthrop said, they came to create "A City Upon a Hill," to serve as a beacon of liberty for the rest of a humanity that was rapidly falling under the domination of the Anglo-Dutch Empire.

Few people today even begin to grasp the profound historical importance of the American Revolution. For Americans, the heritage of that revolution lives on as part of our culture, and the lives of Benjamin Franklin, George Washington, and Abraham Lincoln remain today a living memory within each American citizen. However, over the years, the deeper comprehension of that history has been dulled, as well as deliberately distorted by the Anglophile oligarchy. For others, particularly Europeans, the American Revolution remains a mystery, obscured, as though behind a veil. The long reign of the oligarchy has produced a 21st century Western European culture, in which the oligarchical shackles on the minds of the people have become invisible to the victims, and the Renaissance idea of Commonwealth has become practically incomprehensible. *Most present-day Western Europeans are incapable of seeing that what came into existence between 1775-1787 was not a new nation but a new species of nation.*

America owes its very existence to the breakthroughs in science, technology, music and philosophy which were made possible by the Renaissance, as well as the tremendous courage displayed by many individual Europeans in the 16th, 17th and 18th centuries. Yet, the fact remains, that the endemic power of the European oligarchies prevented a successful "American" revolution from ever being realized on European soil. After the British triumph at the 1815 Congress of Vienna – following more than twenty years of barbaric warfare – the culture of Europe was overwhelmed by a, deliberately fostered, onslaught of existentialism and pessimism. This worsened, dramatically, as a result of the devastation and inhumanity of World War I.

The potential for creating a society based on the actual human identity was diminished, if not eliminated entirely, as the empiricist and reductionist methods of Paolo Sarpi became hegemonic in economics, science, music and all aspects of European culture. Throughout the entirety of the 20th century, the European proponents of the Promethean view of Man have been fighting a rearguard, defensive – and often desperate – battle to keep the human spirit alive.

* * * * *

Most of the 20th Century writings on the American Revolution are just horrible, incompetent, trash. This is particularly true of the Marxist/pseudo-Marxist view of the Revolution as a battle among competing "capitalists." Not surprisingly, the more-recent "neo-con" analysis coheres with that view, as they re-write history to show that the Revolution was a fight against "big government," in favor of libertarian free market values. This is outrageous "snow is black" lying. It's all trash, and not a word of truth in any of it.

Over the last thirty years, the LaRouche political movement has given a gift to humanity, by re-discovering the true history of the founding of the American Republic. A selection of published writings to that end is included in the bibliography to this chapter. These writings demonstrate conclusively that the founding of the United States was the culmination of the Renaissance Commonwealth project. They also dispose of many of the lies routinely taught in university classrooms.

For example, the claim that John Locke was a major influence on the founding of the American republic, is simply untrue, and provably so.[83] It was not the pro-slavery Locke who influenced the founding fathers; it was the networks associated with Gottfried Leibniz – the actual allies of Benjamin Franklin – who provided the political and moral inspiration for the Declaration of Independence and the U.S. Constitution. Among those individuals were Cotton Mather, James Logan, Rudolph Erich Raspe, Baron Gerlach Adolf von Münchausen, Abraham Kästner, Moses Mendelssohn and Gotthold Lessing. These were the individuals who shaped the debate between 1775 and 1787.

In different ways, all of these individuals contributed economic, political, and philosophical ideas that flowed from Leibniz's concept of *happiness*, a concept which Leibniz called "an active and progressive state in which new degrees of perfection are constantly being attained." This concept of Human Happiness – as opposed to the oligarchic

---

[83] See bibliography for: Valenti - *The Anti-Newtonian Roots of the American Revolution*; Shavin - *From Leibniz to Franklin on 'Happiness'*; Trout - *Life, Liberty, and The Pursuit of Happiness: How the Natural Law Concept of Gottfried Wilhelm Leibniz Inspired America's Founding Fathers*

fixation on bestial pleasure – is the distinguishing moral feature of the Commonwealth, as well as the American Republic.

Eleven years before the Declaration of Independence, Raspe published Leibniz's *New Essays on Human Understanding*, the work which destroyed the oligarchic prescriptions of John Locke. It is the precise concept of *human happiness*, which Leibniz discusses in the *New Essays*, that we see enshrined in the words of the Declaration of Independence and the U.S. Constitution.

To repeat, *it is a species difference we are looking at here.* The Sarpi-Descartes-Vitoria-Grotius-Locke-Hobbes-Mandeville-Smith-Malthus-Bentham view of man and society is not just different by degree; it is fundamentally at odds with the republican-Commonwealth concept of the Human Identity. Think of the earlier sections of this work, particularly the words of the apologists of Empire, as you read the following quotations from individuals who actually helped to create the American republic.

Quotations

"You are become a body politic, using among yourselves civil government, and are not furnished with any persons of special eminence above the rest, to be chosen by you into office of government, let your wisdom and godliness appear, not only in choosing such persons as do entirely love and will promote the common good, but also in yielding unto them all due honor and obedience in their lawful administrations..."

John Robinson, Pastor of the Plymouth Church, *Of Faith, Hope, and Love, Reason and Sense* (1620)

Society must be based on "two rules whereby we are to walk one towards another: Justice and Mercy. . . The former derived from the Natural Law of Creation, the latter from the law of grace. . . The care of the public must oversway all private interests."
John Winthrop, *A Model of Christian Charity* (1630)

"It is an invaluable honor to do good; it is an incomparable pleasure. A man must look upon himself as dignified and gratified by God when an  opportunity to do good is placed into his hands. He must embrace it with rapture as enabling him directly to answer the great end of his being. He must manage it with rapturous delight as a most suitable business, as a most precious privilege...we ought to be glad when any opportunity to do good is offered to us. We should need no arguments to make us entertain the offer; but we should naturally fly into the matter as most agreeable to the Divine Nature whereof we are made partakers."
Cotton Mather, *Bonifacius, An Essay upon the Good* (1710)

"But it is the knowledge of necessary and eternal truths which distinguishes us from mere animals, and gives us reason and the sciences, raising us to knowledge of ourselves and God. It is this in us which we call the rational soul or mind...

"Indeed in general I hold that there is nothing truer than happiness, and nothing happier and sweeter than truth." (1670)
Gottfried Leibniz

"Theologian: But what is to love?
"Philosopher: To be delighted by the happiness of another." (1673)
Gottfried Leibniz

"Happiness is the point where center all those duties which individuals and nations owe to themselves; and this is the great end of the law of nature. The desire of happiness is the powerful spring that puts man in motion: felicity is the end they all have in view, and it ought to be the grand object of the public will."
Emmerich de Vattel, *The Law of Nations* (1758)

"The good of man cannot consist in the mere pleasures of sense; because when any one of those objects which you love is absent, or cannot be come at, you are certainly miserable; and if the faculty be impaired, though the object be present, you cannot enjoy it...

"I have showed you what it ("the good") is not. It is not sensual but rational and moral good. It is doing all the good we can to others, by acts of humanity, friendship, generosity, and benevolence; this is that constant and durable good, which will

afford contentment and satisfaction always alike, without variation, and diminution"
> Benjamin Franklin, *Dialogue between Philocles and Horation, Concerning Virtue and Pleasure* (1730)

"We hold these truths to be self-evident, that all men are created equal, that they are endowed by their Creator with certain unalienable Rights, that among these are Life, Liberty and the pursuit of Happiness."
> *The Declaration of Independence*, July 4, 1776

The New Nation

Much has been written about the debates at the 1787 Constitutional Convention, and the ensuing battle to ratify the Constitution, but most of these writings fail to grasp the fundamental principles which constituted the essence of the new nation. The nature of the American Republic is derived from the two greatest principles of the Commonwealth: the concepts of *Sovereignty* and the *General Welfare*. Underlying, and giving purpose to these principles is the moral commitment to the nation's *Posterity*, i.e., an ironclad future-oriented pledge to develop the productive potential of the nation for future generations.

The General Welfare and Sovereignty are inseparable. A defense of the general welfare is impossible without true sovereignty, and sovereignty has no reason for existing except to protect and further the general welfare. Today, "national sovereignty" is routinely denounced by mouthpieces of the oligarchy, like George Soros. It is derided as outmoded and counterposed to "new" ideas like globalization or "universal democracy." "Nationalism" is regularly blamed for all of humanity's past wars. This is not only absurd historical lying, it is a (deliberate) *mis-definition* of the term "sovereignty." Sovereignty does not mean a world governed by individual nations, each of which is engaged in a Hobbesian geo-political competition with other nations, leading to conflict and war. In reality, almost all of the wars of the past two centuries have been caused by the policies of the British Empire, and the idea of encouraging individual nations to fight one another is one of the characteristics of Empire, not of national sovereignty.

More importantly, what is little understood today is the true positive definition of sovereignty. The fundamental idea of sovereignty – the Commonwealth idea of sovereignty – is Sovereignty Over the Oligarchy.

Think of Locke's words in *The Two Treatises of Government*, where he says that oligarchical Private Property Rights are "natural law" rights; that those Property Rights come down to us from Creation; that they pre-date all governments; and that governments exist solely to protect those Property Rights. That is the Empire outlook. That is the outlook of the slave-running and drug-running Dutch and British East India Companies. Sovereignty is the opposite. It is based, in the words of Abraham Lincoln, on the idea of "Government of the people, by the people, and for the people," or, as it is defined in the *Preamble* to the United States Constitution, the General Welfare principle. Sovereignty means, that the nation – *a physical manifestation of the Commonwealth idea –* recognizes no higher, or outside, or supposedly pre-existing entity whose interest is allowed to take precedence over the defense of the General Welfare. The sovereign nation retains the responsibility – *and the full authority –* to defend the General Welfare against all the encroachments of Empire. *That is sovereignty.*

This is why the United States, at least up until our present Bush-Cheney-Obama era, has always been an anticolonial nation. From John Quincy Adams, through Abraham Lincoln, and up to Franklin Roosevelt's battles with Winston Churchill, America was the foremost enemy of colonialism in the world. How could it be otherwise? The Commonwealth idea of the innate dignity of Man, the concept that "all men are created equal," cannot co-exist in a universe where whole categories of human beings are enslaved, exploited, and treated as expendable.

Alexander Hamilton

The Constitution's charge to defend the general welfare is not to be taken as advice to a group of social workers. It means to defend the well-being of the nation – for present and future generations – against oligarchy, and to that end the Constitution grants full sovereign power to our American government over all monetary, credit, and banking policy. No financial oligarchy, no private Central Banking System, is allowed to exert financial or economic power superior to that of government. It is the government, i.e., the elected representatives of the citizens, who will control the economic affairs of the nation, and direct it in such a way as to benefit the Common Good.

Some will charge "That is socialism." No, it is not. It is called the American system of economics, and it all derives from both the intent and authority given within the U.S. Constitution. In 1790 and 1791, Alexander Hamilton – the individual most responsible for the adoption of the U.S. Constitution as well as its final form – authored a series of Reports, wherein he promulgated the revolutionary concept of national *Public Credit.* Hamilton's intention is explicit: to direct the economic affairs of the nation so as to increase the productivity and happiness of the people—to commit the nation to the most rapid scientific, technological and scientific progress; to *create* a better future. This is the economic and philosophical outlook which made America the greatest industrial and scientific power in all of human history. The truth is that there is no such thing as "capitalism." It is a meaningless term. For the last 220 years, human history has been largely determined by a battle between two economic systems: the British (Empire) system of Free Trade and exploitation, and the American system of Public Credit. The United Kingdom and the United States are not two capitalist societies. One is based on the principles of Empire; the other is a constitutional republic based on the Commonwealth Idea.

Under the Empire's private Central Banking System, the individual governments of nations have no sovereign control over their own monetary affairs. They have ceded their power over credit-generation, and even the issuance of money, to private banking interests—to the power of the *fondi.* One of the key methods, by which the oligarchy then controls the destinies of nations is through the issuance of usurious debt, which has no other function but to enrich and enhance the power of the financial oligarchy. Under the American system, it is the government which maintains the sole monopoly right to issue currency, and it is the sovereign credit-generating powers of the government which are used to develop the nation to benefit the Common Good. The evidence of the benefits of this system are abundant throughout the history of the United States, and even today, American schoolchildren are still taught about the building of the Erie Canal, the Transcontinental Railroad, and the Tennessee Valley Authority.

This is a key point. Think back to the discussions earlier in this work concerning the subject of money. For John Locke, and the rest, money is a self-evident thing. It exists, as an independent entity, within the invisible "free market." This free market system of money exists independent of all governments. Governments can only get access to this money by borrowing, taxation, or other means, and only under conditions allowed by the Central Banking System. Contrary to this, in the United States, Constitutionally, money has no independent existence whatsoever. It is a product – a tool – of the credit-generating power of the government. Hamilton's system is a sovereign credit system, not a money system.

The economic policies of Empire – as we have seen increasingly since 1971 – create monopolies, particularly financial monopolies, with power concentrated in fewer and fewer hands. The livelihoods, and productive powers, of the vast majority of people are driven downwards, again, as we have witnessed since 1971. The American Republic, as Roosevelt challenged Churchill in 1945, is one that is Constitutionally mandates to uplift its people, utilizing sovereign power to regulate and direct financial practices to the benefit of all.

Protectionism

Consider the following quote from Henry Carey, writing in *Financial Crises: Their Cause and Effects*:

"The history of the Union for the past half century may now briefly thus be stated: We have had three periods of protection, closing in 1817, 1834, and

1847, each and all of them leaving the country in a state of the highest prosperity - competition for the purchase of labor then growing daily and rapidly, with constant tendency towards increase in the amount of commerce, in the steadiness of the societary action, and in the freedom of the men who needed to sell their labor.

"We have had three periods of that system which looks to the destruction of domestic commerce, and is called free trade-that system which prevails in Ireland and India, Portugal and Turkey, and is advocated by British journalists-each and all of them having led to crises such as you have so well described, to wit, in 1822, 1842, and 1857. In each and every case, they have left the country in a state of paralysis, similar to that which now exists

"Turn to the years which followed the abandonment of the protective policy in 1816, and study the rapid growth of pauperism and wretchedness that was then observed. Pass on to those which followed the passage of the protective tariffs of 1824 and 1828, and remark the wonderful change towards wealth and freedom that was at once produced. Study next the growth of pauperism and destitution under the compromise tariff, closing with the almost entire paralysis of 1840-42. Pass onward, and examine the action of the tariff of 1842 - remarking the constant increase in the demand for labor-in the production and consumption of iron, and of cotton and woolen goods-and in the strength and power of a community which had so recently been obliged to apply, and that in vain, at all the banking houses of Europe, for the small amount of money that then was needed for carrying on the government.

"Pauperism, slavery, and crime, as you have seen, follow everywhere in the train of the British free-trade system....."

Today, it is routine for mouthpieces of the Empire to attack protectionism as outmoded and in violation of the principles of globalization. But consider two things: first, that the United States is constitutionally a protectionist system, and second, that protectionism is not simply a matter of protectionist tariffs. "Protectionism" defines a broader commitment to the industrial, scientific, and educational development of the nation. It defines a "protectionist" approach toward the well-being of the current and future generations. It entails a commitment to infrastructure development. It defines a capital intensive development of the physical economy, and the uplifting of the skills and educational levels of the citizenry. This is, of course the opposite of the "buy cheap – sell dear" free trade policies of Adam Smith and the British Empire.

The idea is to *Protect the People* against the financial oligarchy and to build for a better future.

The *Intention* of the American Public Credit system is to be found in Alexander Hamilton's 1791 *Report on Manufacturers* and in his creation of the First National Bank of the United States. Unfortunately, most academics who study Hamilton's writings fail, once again, to think through what is actually being discussed is the moral and scientific question as to the nature of Man, what it actually means to be a human being.

What Hamilton posits is a continual improvement, an uplifting of the human condition, an approach which will lead to an increase in national and individual productivity, all accomplished through willful creative discoveries and inventions,—and his system of Public Credit is designed to foster such positive development. This all rests on a foundation of understanding human nature as inherently *creative*, as absolutely distinguished from the lower beasts. And this is in direct violent opposition to the oligarchical view of humanity. What Hamilton envisioned was a Republic which operated from this philosophical view of human potential.

Unfortunately, after Hamilton's murder – and with the sole exception of the nation-builder John Quincy Adams – America largely abandoned Hamilton's outlook and policies. They were not fully eradicated, because the purpose and experience of the American Revolution was still a living influence, and the principles in the Constitution and the Declaration of Independence still acted as a guidepost for the nation, but as the 19th century progressed America most certainly lost its way. This included the lunatic anti-Hamilton banking and monetary policies of Presidents Jackson and Van Buren, as well as the rapid expansion of the British Empire-created slave system throughout large parts of the nation.

In 1861, President Abraham Lincoln revived Hamilton's approach, with a policy of high protective tariffs, the issuance of a national currency ("Greenbacks"), and in-depth development of the productive powers of the economy, typified by such projects as the Transcontinental Railroad.[84]

In the 1890's, President William McKinley would implement the highest protective tariff in American history, and later, during the crisis of the 1930's Franklin Roosevelt would return to the policies of Hamilton, Carey, Lincoln, and McKinley in his measures to take sovereign control over

---

[84] For the implementation of Hamiltonian economic policies by the Lincoln administration, see *The Civil War and the American System,* by Alan Salisbury

U.S. monetary and credit policy, and to implement measures to rebuild the nation.

Exemplary of Roosevelt's approach are his 1933 actions to de-link from the British Gold Standard and reorganize the banking system, as well as his use of the credit-generating powers of the government – e.g., through the Reconstruction Finance Corporation – and his deployment of Harry Hopkins to unleash a massive rebuilding and improvement of the nation's internal infrastructure.

All of this, from Hamilton through Roosevelt, was done by utilizing the sovereign power of national government to direct economic and financial policy to serve the Common Good.

Empire against the Commonwealth

From the earliest days, the London based Empire was determined to destroy the potential for a Commonwealth in America. Throughout the 17th century there were continuous economic and political attacks on the New England colonies. This culminated in 1684 when the Crown revoked Massachusetts' colonial Charter, and then, in 1686, imposed on Massachusetts a Royal Governor. This situation worsened after the Dutch takeover of England in 1688, with the creation of John Locke's Board of Trade and Plantations, and the founding of the New East India Company. The coronation of the Hanoverian George I in 1714 resulted in yet more repression against the colonies. These were not "disputes" between Boston and London merchants. Recall that this was the period of British domination of the world slave trade, and the beginnings of mass opium production in India. That future is what the colonists resisted.

After the American victory in the Revolutionary War, the British made repeated attempts over the next 80 years to destroy the new nation. These included Aaron Burr's British-backed treason, the London-directed destruction of Hamilton's national banking system (including Martin Van Buren's insane policy of "free banking"), and the London-controlled insurrection known as the "Civil War."

As a result of the Union victory in the Civil War, after 1865, and particularly after 1876, the methods of American economics spread all over the world. Japan, China, Germany, Russia, and other nations rebelled against the British policies of Free Trade, and began to develop their economies, using protective tariffs to encourage industry and constructing large-scale infrastructure projects.

Throughout the 19th century, the London-based system of Empire relentlessly pursued the expansion of its global reach, imposing ever more death and destruction, as described in the previous chapter of this work. Agents of the Empire – such as Jeremy Bentham and John Stuart Mill – in their writings on utilitarianism,[85] proclaimed that the philosophy of this Empire would not be the Commonwealth/Leibnizian notion of the "pursuit of happiness," but instead the "pursuit of pleasure," as defined earlier by the enemy of America, Adam Smith, in his *Theory of Moral Sentiments*. Thus, they justified the greatest global looting in history.

Franklin Roosevelt

To conclude this chapter, it is important to make a few brief remarks about the Presidency of Franklin Delano Roosevelt. Foolish present-day populists, who decry

---

[85] *An Introduction to the Principles of Morals and Legislation*, by Jeremy Bentham, 1781, published by Batoche Books, Kitchener, 2000

Roosevelt as an "internationalist" or "socialist," are simply

incredibly clueless, and if one digs deep enough you will find that most of such critics of Roosevelt are devotees of the British Empire's "Austrian School" of oligarchical monetarism. This is unbelievably shallow thinking, wherein there is a complete failure to distinguish between oligarchical worshipers of money versus the Renaissance Commonwealth Principle of America.

Following the speculative financial binges of the 1920's, Franklin Roosevelt's campaign in defense of the *Forgotten Man* was a trumpet, heralding a return to the Constitutional principle of the General Welfare. Every action Roosevelt took demonstrated a deep-rooted patriotic commitment to the absolute sovereignty of the nation, beginning with his break with the British Gold Standard in 1933.

Roosevelt's bank reorganization, his regulation of the financial markets through such measures as the 1933 Glass-Steagall Act and the 1934 creation of the Securities and Exchange Commission, and his actions against commodity speculation all demonstrate the proper role of a sovereign government, acting on behalf of the Common Good. One example of such sovereign action was Roosevelt's 1936 creation of the Commodity Exchange Administration, which imposed federal regulation on all financial "futures trading," and outlawed completely all "options trading" (a ban lasting until 1981).

Simultaneous with his attacks on financial and commodity speculation, Roosevelt acted to expand the nation's productive capabilities. The Reconstruction Finance Corporation, the Works Progress Administration, and other agencies all utilized government generated credit to carry out tens of thousands of construction projects in the United States. Schools, bridges, hospitals, canals, irrigation projects, flood control projects, dams, port facilities, and highways were built by the hundreds. Rural electrification was accomplished. The great "Four Corners" projects (including the Tennessee Valley and the Colombia River projects) were built.

Farmers were guaranteed a fair price through the Roosevelt farm "parity" policy. The elderly were rescued from destitution by Social Security. Labor reform gave working people the right to fight for a livable wage. Health care reform, which eventually resulted in the Hill-Burton legislation, ensured medical care for all Americans, regardless of income.

Do not confuse any of this with the European idea of the "welfare state." Roosevelt's accomplishments, and methods, are derived directly from Alexander Hamilton, Henry Carey, and Abraham Lincoln. This was the American Constitutional economic system, both in its intent and its actions. This was our government acting as it was intended to act, a sovereign power acting on behalf of the General Welfare and against the financial power of Empire.

XII. Chapter 12 - Richard Nixon's blunder: the post-1971 world

Oakland, California - summer, 2018

The history of the United States since Franklin Roosevelt's final reelection campaign, in 1944, contains all of the elements of a Shakespearean tragedy. But this tragedy is not fictitious, nor merely appearing on a stage; it is in the real lives we all live day to day. From the greatest power in the world in 1944, we have seen America's sovereign powers surrendered; we have seen an almost shattered British Empire rise again, to threaten global destruction on a scale never before realized; and we have seen our people become smaller, lose their sense of history, and be increasingly corrupted by the ever-pervasive oligarchical culture within which we exist.

The death of Franklin Roosevelt in 1945 was a catastrophe for humanity. Within days of Roosevelt's death, the fool Harry Truman abandoned Roosevelt's post-war intention to dismantle the British, French, and Dutch Empires,[86] and instead, he joined with those reconstituted empires, in subjugating the United States to the British Empire's "cold war" confrontation with the Soviet Union. Roosevelt's anti-imperial policy was replaced by increasing American subservience to a pro-imperial "special relationship" with the British Empire.

In 1963, the assassination of Roosevelt-admirer President John F. Kennedy took America another ratchet downward. The era of the John F. Kennedy who pledged to put men on the moon "within this decade," was followed

---

[86] For Roosevelt's fight with Winston Churchill on ending the British Empire, see *As He Saw It,* by Elliott Roosevelt

instead by the decade of the Vietnam War, and the eruption of the baby-boomer, pleasure-oriented, drug counterculture. America was plunged into an era of pleasure-seeking pessimism, from which it has yet to recover. From being a republic which was always *future-oriented*, America has become a nation without a mission.

1971

From the standpoint of sovereign economic policy, Richard Nixon's August 15, 1971 abolition of Franklin Roosevelt's Bretton Woods Monetary System was the ultimate turning point, a decision which opened the floodgates for the Empire to reassert its global financial power. All of the economic woes we suffer today can be traced to that calamitous policy shift. The fixed-exchange rate Bretton Woods system, which functioned as an agreement among sovereign governments to ensure monetary stability, to provide regulatory restraints on financial speculation, and to create a sound environment for long term economic investment and real economic development, was replaced by a new paradigm of free trade, globalization, deregulation, financial speculation, and oligarchic efforts to destroy national sovereignty.

The historical disaster of Nixon's 1971 action was followed in short order by the 1973 "oil crisis," which was then used to destroy America's sovereign control over her own currency. The way this worked has been described by Lyndon LaRouche:[87]

"The effect of the oil shortage was to create the spot market, and under the spot market, the U.S. dollar became a creature of petroleum... Before that event,

---

[87] Lyndon LaRouche International Webcast, "Averting Doom," March 12, 2008,

the spot market, based in Amsterdam, had been a very minor part of the world petroleum marketing. The effect of this, was to make the dollar, which was still being used, no longer really a U.S. dollar internationally: It became an Anglo-American dollar, a "petrodollar"... As a result of this combination, the floating of the U.S. dollar, by President Nixon, and the spot market, the security of the U.S. dollar was no longer based on the value of the U.S. dollar, but it was based on the fluctuating value of petroleum... Both events are being steered from London, not from the United States, but from London. Both represent the fact that, especially since 1971, the United States' dollar has nominally been a leading factor in the world, but it has not been a U.S. dollar, it has been an international dollar... And in this process, you had a fundamental shift occurring, between 1968 and 1975, in which, instead of having the nations of Europe and the United States as being the prime drivers of the world physical economy, there was now a great shift in progress."

An important component of the "great shift" which LaRouche references was the move towards an open neo-colonial economic policy. Key to this process was the 1986-1994 Uruguay Round discussions of the GATT (General Agreement on Trades and Tariffs) organization, which culminated in the founding of the World Trade Organization in 1995. Under the WTO policy direction of the past 13 years, we have witnessed an ongoing destruction of the productive powers of labor in both the advanced sector nations as well as in the developing sector. The Hamilton-Lincoln-Roosevelt policy of nation-building has been replaced, on a global scale, with the "buy cheap-sell dear" regime of Adam Smith and the British East India Company. The productive economies of Europe and North America have been destroyed, while Mexico, Asia, Africa and elsewhere have become the locations of virtual slave-labor maquiladoras, and related economic "investments."

Under this new Empire globalist regime, national food self-sufficiency has been destroyed in dozens of countries, by a lack of investment, and a policy of shifting out of food production into producing "cash crops" for export. Across the globe, millions of peoples' basic right of access to food is now determined by a handful of international cartels, and the policies of the WTO.

This has all been accompanied by the imposition of a vast system of global usury, forced down the throats of those nations least of capable resisting it. The International Monetary Fund, an agency created as part of the Bretton Woods agreement to be the vehicle for sovereign government oversight over world financial affairs, has been transformed, since 1971, into a creature of the Empire. Working with private banks and independent "vulture funds," the IMF has ensnared dozens of nations in a web of usurious debt, which is then used to impose demands for brutal economic austerity, and a further surrender of national sovereignty. John Perkins' book provides useful insights into the deliberate intent governing those actions.[88]

What of the United States itself? Since 1971, we've lost most of our industry; our current health care system is a crime against humanity; our national infrastructure—including energy, fresh water and transportation—is collapsing; real physical living standards have declined; and our banking system has been transformed into an enormous gambling casino, which now teeters on the brink of collapse and ruin. In addition, and perhaps most

---

[88] *Confessions of an Economic Hitman,* by John Perkins

ominous for the future of the nation, Britain's new Opium War against the United States has now ensnared two to three generations of Americans in a now near-hegemonic drug culture.

The return of the Ridotto

The government of Venice closed the famous *Ridotto* casino in 1774, after most of the Venetian aristocracy had gambled themselves into penury. Somehow the lesson of that fiasco has been lost on the Barney "bailout" Franks of today.

Richard Nixon's criminal actions of 1971 opened the door to allow the financial oligarchy to transform the entire U.S. financial and banking system into one big gambling casino, and to bring in the same financial methods which led to previous centuries' speculative catastrophes, such as the John Law and South Sea bubbles.[89]

In 1973 the Chicago Board of Trade opened its "Options Exchange," which initiated trades in European-style financial options for the first time since such trading was made illegal by Franklin Roosevelt in 1936.[90] That same year the "Black-Scholes Formula" was published in the *Journal of Political Economy*. Using mathematical formulas to "predict" market behavior, use of the Black-Scholes and related methods quickly spread throughout the financial community, as the preferred technique to engage in financial gambling.[91]

---

[89] *Yes! It Really is Gambling*, by Robert Ingraham, op. cit.

[90] It was the Chicago Board of Trade which originally initiated London-style futures and options trading in the United States in 1865, only months after Abraham Lincoln's assassination. This speculative activity flourished until Franklin Roosevelt banned most of these practices in 1936.

[91] It was the same Fisher Black, who in 1985, developed the "Black-Derman-Toy" model which led to the rapid expansion of trading in financial derivatives.

In 1974, Franklin Roosevelt's Commodity Exchange Administration was abolished and replaced by the pro-speculation Commodity Futures Trading Commission (CFTC). Between 1974 and 1982, the CFTC legalized (or acquiesced in the creation of) a variety of speculative financial instruments, including currency futures, interest rate futures, and stock index futures. In 1982 Congress passed the Futures Trading Act, which officially legalized options trading, and expanded the role of the CFTC at the expense of the Roosevelt-created Securities and Exchange Commission, giving the pro-speculation CFTC sole oversight over all commodity futures and options trading.

In 1988, Wendy Gramm, the wife of Sen. Phil Gramm (R-Tex.), was appointed chairman of the CFTC. Under her leadership, the floodgates were opened for a massive growth of the derivatives market.

In 1992, Enron was allowed by the Gramm-led CFTC to remove energy derivatives and interest-rate swaps from CFTC oversight. This opened the door to a new era of profiteering in the energy markets.

In 1994, Long Term Capital Management (LTCM) hedge fund is started up by Robert C. Merton and Myron S. Scholes. Using the Black-Scholes "method," the collapse of LTCM in 1998 almost brought down the entire banking system.

In 1999, Congress repealed the Roosevelt-era Glass-Steagall Act, opening the door for the federally-chartered commercial banks to engage in the same speculative practices as the investment banks.

In 2000, Congress passed the Commodities Futures Modernization Act, which expanded the power of the CFTC, repealed the laws against stock futures, and – most importantly – liberalized the regulations against the insane Over-the-Counter (OTC) derivatives.

As a result of these actions, following the stock market crash of 1987, and under the "guidance" of Fed chairmen Alan "wall of money" Greenspan and Ben "bubbles" Bernanke, America embarked on a speculative binge unprecedented in human history, resulting in the dot-com crash of 2000-2001, the mortgage crash of 2007, and the looming banking crash we face today. Current news headlines concerning the insolvency of Bear Stearns, Indy Mac, Fannie Mae, and Freddie Mac, are just the canary in the coal mine. Over the past 30 years our entire banking system, a system vital to the national security of the nation, has been bankrupted and destroyed. There is no saving it within the existing financial axioms of Empire.

Fascism & Hope

The deliberate destruction of America's industrial economy and banking institutions is just the beginning of the story. What humanity is now facing is not simply a financial collapse, per se, but a civilizational collapse, the destruction of all nation states and a degeneration into a global new dark age.

If you think that statement is extreme, look at what has transpired over the past 15 years, and where we find ourselves today:

1)   In the absence of any assertion of national sovereignty, control over the world money markets has shifted almost entirely into private hands. A crucial step towards that end was the setting up of the offshore financial centers, beginning in the 1990s. Located primarily in British Crown Colonies, such as the Cayman Islands, Bermuda, and the British Virgin Islands, as well as select other locations like the Dutch Antilles, these oligarchical entities have become the home of thousands of hedge funds, private equity funds, and other unregulated financial activity. The Cayman Islands, alone, is home to over 8,000 hedge funds, and its banking system holds $1.4 trillion in deposits, making it the fourth-largest banking center in the world, after the U.S.A., Japan, and Britain.

These Anglo-Dutch Empire enclaves operate outside the control of any sovereign government. They are completely unregulated, and their financial records are held in strict secrecy. All of these centers have become the loci of massive drug-money laundering and financial speculation. Swarming out of the crevices of these Empire nests, the financial vultures speculate on food, oil, and other resources. They carry out attacks on the currencies of nations, and buy up and dismantle whole chunks of the productive economy in the United States and elsewhere.

2) In tandem with this creation of the Empire's offshore financial operations, has come a concerted drive to place control over world trade and key commodities, including food, oil, strategic metals, pharmaceuticals, etc., under the dominance of a relative handful of global corporations, which work in sync with the Empire's financial centers. In 1968, at a meeting of the Bilderberg Group in Mont Tremblant, Canada, former Lehman Brothers banker George Ball called for the creation of what he called the World Company.

As John Hoefle described this project:[92]

> "The aim of this "world company" project, as explained by Ball, was to eliminate 'the archaic political structure of the nation state' in favor of a more "modern" corporate structure. The world

---

[92] *Fascism and the Project For a World Company*, by John Hoefle, EIR

company has a great potential for good as an instrument for efficiently utilizing resources,' Ball said... The idea was explicitly Malthusian, based upon the claim that the combination of global overpopulation and a shortage of natural resources required a more efficient management process than nations, with their political biases, could provide... As we have indicated in numerous locations, what is being proposed is a form of Mussolini-style corporatism, in which government becomes the agent for rule by financier-run corporate cartels."

What we are witnessing here is the rebirth, in modern garb, of the British and Dutch East India Companies. This process began with the corporate mergers and acquisitions of the 1980s and 1990s, much of which were funded by the British offshore financial centers, but what we are seeing today is no longer merely "corporate takeovers," but the increasing cartelization of the entire world economy and banking houses, into fewer and fewer private oligarchical hands. The present proposal in the United States, to hand whole sections of our federally-regulated banking system over to the private equity funds, and to eliminate most government oversight and regulation, is part of this cartelization process. For the individuals involved in this scheme, national sovereignty no longer exists. It is, in essence, a global system, "of the oligarchy, by the oligarchy, and for the oligarchy," in which governments are reduced to merely the servants of that oligarchy. This is the modern Anglo-Dutch Empire.

3) **The British Empire policies of genocide and permanent war, described in Chapter 11 of this work, are now being recreated on a global scale.** Consider what was reported on British mass murder in India, and look at what we are seeing today.

According to a press release issued by Oxfam International on July 23, 2008, more than 15 million East Africans are at risk of "severe hunger and destitution" within months. They report that the cost of food has risen "500% in some places" causing "utter destitution." Oxfam found the cost of imported rice to Somalia soared 350% between January 2007 and May 2008, and 35 percent of the population requires food aid. All the Horn of Africa countries, Kenya, Ethiopia, Somalia, Eritrea, and Djibouti are desperate. In Ethiopia the price of wheat doubled in six months and 10 million people face starvation. An Oxfam spokesman described witnessing a road "littered with dead livestock" and people grinding "food pellets intended for their animals" to make "porridge to feed their families."

This is not a crisis limited to Africa. There have been food riots in Haiti, Egypt, India, and dozens of countries around the world. Vulture speculators have driven up the price of food, and nations which were once self-sufficient in food production, are now helpless, after the last 20 years of free trade and cartelization of global food production.

As nation-states disintegrate, chaos and war are the result. This intended result, is then used as the excuse for global imperial wars, some utilizing East-India Company-style private mercenary armies, and others involving American and European "rapid deployment" and other "special ops" forces, deployed on behalf of the Empire. To accomplish this, the people of the United States and Europe are given a series of "enemy images," which supposedly represent threats to our security, e.g. Iraq, Iran, Sudan, Zimbabwe, North Korea, etc. This "enemy image" methodology is no different then the pablum served up to the people of England in the 19th century to justify

England's colonial wars. And of course the real enemy of our Republic, the Empire, is never mentioned.

Even worse, the present existential crisis within the world financial system, and the threat that nations will respond to this crisis by reasserting national sovereignty, is impelling the British Empire to unleash global strategic war, as they did in 1914. That threat is now real and growing.

* * * * *

The material contained in this chapter was written fourteen years ago, and as stated in the Introduction to this work, a lot has changed during those years. Since then the global economic and financial crisis has worsened dramatically. The political crisis has also deepened. Yet many nations are fighting for a future and significant economic development projects have been undertaken. Among these are those associated with China's Belt and Road Initiative, a project involving now dozens of sovereign nations to build desperately needed economic development projects throughout the world. These include fresh water projects, high speed rail, nuclear power plants, new ports, new cities and other physical transformations.

What stated here, however, should not be read as an uncritical endorsement of China's political system, its economic system, nor of the ultimate viability of the Belt and Road Project itself. Rather, it merely signifies the yearning of nations to free themselves from imperial financial rule.

More importantly, we are beginning to witness a growing potential for cooperation among the major sovereign nations of the world—including, but not limited to, the United States, Russia, India and China—focused on building up the physical economic potentials of these nations, including nuclear power, water development, transportation and city-building.   What is most important – what is crucial – is that projects are being built!   Human lives are being improved. Scientific frontiers are being explored. And this is all being done outside of and in opposition to the financial institutions of the Anglo-Dutch Empire.

As for our own United States of America, we find ourselves at a fork in the road. As Lyndon LaRouche emphasized in his July 22, 2008 International Webcast, there is absolutely no hope of saving the present world monetary system. There are no "reforms" that are going to work. We have but two choices: the pathway defined by the Empire, or a return to the sovereign economic methods of

Lyndon H. LaRouche, Jr.

Alexander Hamilton, Abraham Lincoln, and Franklin Roosevelt.   All of the tools required to choose the second path still exist in the sovereign constitutional powers of the United States government. Willing allies exist, including China, Russia, India, and many other nations, to bring into existence new financial and economic agreements. The concrete steps taken by Franklin Roosevelt still exist as a matter of historical record, waiting to be put into practice again today. The initial steps required to begin an economic recovery also exist, to be found in both Lyndon LaRouche's March, 2008 "Three Steps to Survival," as well as his June, 2014 "Four New Laws to Save the U.S.A. Now!"[93] These

---

[93] available at the LaRouche PAC website

provide a clear starting point for reversing the economic collapse and returning to sane traditional economic principles. The solution to the current global financial and monetary breakdown crisis also exists in the form of LaRouche's proposal for a New Bretton Woods Monetary System, a proposal first enunciated by LaRouche in March of 1998, and still awaiting action today.

The solutions are all available. What's required is the will to act. What's missing is individual courage. This is the issue on which this present work began. History doesn't happen. It is voluntaristic. We are faced with a life-and-death crisis. What are we going to do about it? If enough of us act now, if we can find in ourselves the same historical courage as the soldiers at Valley Forge, or the same determination to save the principles of 1776 as Presidents Lincoln and Roosevelt, then time still exists to win this fight. But time is running short.

~

Appendix 1 – Keynes or Hayek?

Feb. 23, 2018—It is time to free the minds of the American people from the shackles of British Economics. This is not an academic issue, to be confined only to the classroom. Over the recent decades, America—together with most of Western Europe—has become a shell of its former industrial, technological and scientific greatness, while poverty, drug addiction and homelessness have spread unchecked.

Unfortunately, Congressional, as well as popular, debates on economic policy are now almost always, at best, uninformed, and usually based on wildly false assumptions and ignorance. There is an ongoing phony confrontation between "left" and "right" with heated assertions from both sides—while the actual fundamental issues are almost never discussed. One hears the opposing sides yapping at each other all the time: "privatization" versus state ownership; regulation versus deregulation; tax cuts versus tax increases; "freedom" versus "socialism." That is the debate as it is presented to everyone, and the only choice you are given is to pick a "side." But is that really true?

Today, many believe—erroneously—that there is a fundamental principled difference between those who believe in "less government" and those who believe in "big government." This is often represented as a debate between "personal freedom" versus "statist" control, with the "Austrian School" of Ludwig von Mises and Friedrich Hayek representing the former, and John Maynard Keynes the latter.

For those who believe in such a schema, or even worse, have chosen sides in this "debate," there is only one thing that can be said: You have been fooled. You are the victim of a massive swindle, the intention of which is to hide from you the nature of real physical economics. You have been given a contrived choice between two London-created pessimistic ideologies, neither of which will lead to an improvement in the human condition.

Sucking on Britain's Teat

In 1758, Adam Smith published *The Theory of Moral Sentiments*, followed in 1776 by his *An Inquiry into the Nature and Causes of the Wealth of Nations*. Although some readers may react with outrage, it must be stated, unequivocally, that these two works present a moral philosophy and a system of economics absolutely hostile to the intention of the American Revolution. If you worship Adam Smith, you understand neither George Washington, nor the U.S. Constitution's *Preamble*.

All of Smith's economics proceeds, lawfully, from a pessimistic, bestial view of human nature. Smith is explicit that he views humankind as a swarm of creatures governed by selfish, sensual impulses, greed, and the "pursuit of pleasure and avoidance of pain," to use his own words. For Smith, the purpose of a monetary and commercial system is to increase human pleasure, and that increase in pleasure can be accomplished only through the accumulation of "wealth," which he defines strictly in monetary terms, i.e., through profits derived from financial speculation or through the trade in monetarily denominated goods. This is the basis for Smith's notion of the "great mercantile republic," whereby, through buying and selling commodities and financial contracts (i.e., "buying cheap and selling dear"), monetary wealth might be accumulated.

This deliberate mis-identifying of "money" with "wealth" is not an error that George Washington, Abraham Lincoln, Alexander Hamilton or John Quincy Adams would have fallen into. Read Lincoln's 1858 lecture, "Discoveries and Inventions," where he is explicit that the sole source of all actual human wealth—all human happiness—lies in the power of the human mind to make new discoveries, i.e., to create revolutionary breakthroughs which transform human productivity and enhance human progress.

The United Kingdom has always been an empire based both on oligarchical rule and a monetary notion of wealth. Following Adam Smith, in the early to mid-19th Century, London became the center for what is sometimes called "British Liberal Economics," often identified with the likes of Jeremy Bentham, Parson Thomas Malthus, James Mill, Mill's son John Stuart Mill, and Richard Cobden. It is precisely that 19th century British Liberalism which is the common mother to the siblings Keynes and Hayek.

The primary issue of true economics is the necessity to increase human productivity, to increase mankind's mastery over the planet, and to unlock the mysteries of the universe. Where is that imperative to be found in either Keynes or in the Austrian School? Nowhere! Yet, that imperative is the basis for all human progress, and indeed the continued survival of the human species. Instead, Keynes and Hayek both start with the identical ironclad axioms postulated by Smith: 1) Man is a creature governed by his sensual passions, and 2) Those impulses can be satiated only through an accumulation of wealth (money). All that Hayek and Keynes disagree on is the method by which that oligarchical diktat might best be realized. It is a debate over method, not intent.

Deluded fools sometimes argue that the pursuit of such monetary "wealth" might collectively benefit the Common Good. That was certainly Smith's argument, one he copied from Bernard Mandeville's 1714 *Fable of the Bees*. Victims of that outlook might be advised to begin reading the *New Testament*, for nowhere in that book will they find postulated the idea that accumulated evil can produce good. Only a fool would buy into an argument grounded in such moral turpitude.

In 1931, Friedrich Hayek responded to the 1930 publication of John Maynard Keynes' *A Treatise on Money*, with a series of lectures at the London School of Economics, delivering a critique which eviscerated Keynes's work. Down to the present day, that debate between Keynes and Hayek—a debate which occurred *within* the imperial British establishment—has been dictated throughout academic circles as the only acceptable basis for discussing economic and monetary policy. This is the only choice you are given— between Keynes and Hayek, or some variation—and the subservience of both men to the financial empire based in London is never mentioned.

Mathematics & Madness

Even worse, flowing from the influence of David Hilbert, Bertrand Russell, and John von Neumann, we now live in the era of "mathematical economics," one wherein the "monetary" theories of Keynes, Hayek, et al. have been merged with the linear mathematical methods of Russell. Money and the accumulation of monetary wealth are the goal, and ever more sophisticated mathematical formulas are the means to achieve that goal. At the center of this is statistical probability theory, another subject about which both Keynes and the Austrians (through the person of Richard von Mises, Ludwig's brother) wrote major works.

Although it is beyond the scope of this article, it is important to note that on the subjects of money, mathematics, and probability theory, much of the oligarchical ground-work goes back to earlier centuries, to individuals such as Bacon, Newton, Hobbes, Locke and Hume; and even earlier these matters were subjects of intense deliberation in Amsterdam, the financial capital of the Dutch Empire. The roots for all of this flow from an anti-human imperial oligarchical outlook, stretching back over centuries.

The belief in money and the various schemes to manipulate it in order to accumulate "wealth," is most assuredly a form of mental illness. It is no different from the fever which takes control of the "card counter" in Las Vegas, or the "day trader," who plugs in a mathematical formula to make a killing in the market. The lottery ticket buyer with his or her "system" falls into the same category. Yet, this is the methodology now hegemonic on Wall Street, in government agencies, in university classrooms, and throughout most of the general public.

Creating Something New

If you want to truly understand how a given society can willfully progress to a future higher level, it is necessary to begin with Gottfried Leibniz' writings on Physical (not "monetary") Economics. The next step is to read Alexander Hamilton's *Report on the Subject of Manufactures*. Studying the presidencies of Abraham Lincoln and Franklin Roosevelt also helps. Finally, take up the study of Lyndon LaRouche's writings, perhaps beginning with *So You Wish to Learn All About Economics*.

Man is the only creature capable of altering his relation with nature; the only creature capable of willfully increasing its per-capita population density; the only creature which progresses. None of this has to do with the manipulation of money.

To again reference Abraham Lincoln, the secret to human progress (and happiness) is to be found in his 1858 lecture, "Discoveries and Inventions." Our ability to make scientific breakthroughs and to use those breakthroughs to accomplish an upward (sometimes revolutionary) shift in the condition of the human species, is unique to mankind, and it is the real subject of economics. It is the only real subject of economics. The issue is human creativity, which generates just such potential progress. Such creativity, such progress is the only basis for optimism, for actual sanity, because it is the only approach which is future-oriented.

Today, there is a great deal of debate about "private versus public" investment, and controversies around issues such as "tax cuts." The lunacy of much of the chatter surrounding these matters is revealed by the reality that almost all those involved accept the monetarist axioms of economics which were created in London.

Take the example of Gross Domestic Product as a supposed measurement of national economic wealth. This actually originated in a 1665 writing of the British aristocrat Sir William Petty, titled *Verbum Sapienti*. Therein, Petty attempted to define the national wealth of Great Britain by assigning everything in the country a monetary value: land, sheep, salt, housing, ships, etc.—even people. But what does that get you? What truth does it contain? How do you get from there into a better future?

There is only one yardstick for judging correct versus incorrect economic policy. Are the initiatives you are taking (as a nation) and the projects you are funding, going to produce an effect of increasing the productivity of the nation? Will your actions increase energy utilization per-capita? Will they increase potential relative population density? Will they have the effect of uplifting the conditions and cognitive potential of the population Will all of this benefit our posterity?

Any other approach is sterile, dead, and fraudulent. Don't get fooled (i.e., be foolish) into "right versus left" scenarios. If the government can get the job done, good. If the private sector can get the job done, good. If selective tax cuts work, do it. If selective tax increases work, do that. If government regulations serve a useful purpose, keep them; if, instead, they are used—as in the case of the Environmental Protection Agency—to enforce a Malthusian agenda, get rid of them. The only goal is upward progress. Break out of the Keynes-versus-Hayek mental prison of monetarism.

This is precisely where the issue of Hamiltonian Public Credit comes in. Public Credit is not European Central Banking. It is not the Federal Reserve. It is precisely, the elected representatives of the American people, acting through a government-chartered corporation, to ensure that the surplus wealth of the nation is put to constructive work to develop infrastructure, science, technology and other projects which will carry the nation into the future. Hamilton's system of Public Credit is the only approach which has been historically proven to be capable of accomplishing that goal.

There is daunting work to be done to "Make America Great Again." We need to build great projects. We need an economic approach which will succeed. We need to build for the future, not simply make money.

Appendix 2 – Selections from Franklin Roosevelt

Address Accepting the Presidential Nomination at the Democratic National Convention in Chicago, July 2nd, 1932

"There are two ways of viewing the Government's duty in matters affecting economic and social life. The first sees to it that a favored few are helped and hopes that some of their prosperity will leak through, sift through, to labor, to the farmer, to the small business man. That theory belongs to the party of Toryism, and I had hoped that most of the Tories left this country in 1776

"Yes, the people of this country want a genuine choice this year, not a choice between two names for the same reactionary doctrine. Ours must be a party of liberal thought, of planned action, of enlightened international outlook, and of the greatest good to the greatest number of our citizens.

"Now it is inevitable--and the choice is that of the times--it is inevitable that the main issue of this campaign should revolve about the clear fact of our economic condition, a depression so deep that it is without precedent in modern history."

First Inaugural Address, March 4, 1933

"In such a spirit on my part, and on yours, we face our common difficulties. They concern, thank God, only material things. Values have shrunken to fantastic levels; taxes have risen; our ability to pay has fallen; government of all kinds is faced by serious curtailment of income; the means of exchange are frozen in the currents of trade; the withered leaves of industrial enterprise lie on every side; farmers find no markets for their produce; the savings of many years in thousands of families are gone...

"Primarily this is because the rulers of the exchange of mankind's goods have failed, through their own stubbornness and their own incompetence, have admitted their failure, and abdicated. Practices of the unscrupulous money-changers stand indicted in the court of public opinion, rejected by the hearts and minds of men...

"True they have tried, but their efforts have been cast in the pattern of an outworn tradition. Faced by failure of credit they have proposed only the lending of more money. Stripped of the lure of profit by which to induce our people to follow their false leadership, they have resorted to exhortations, pleading tearfully for restored confidence. They know only the rules of a generation of self-seekers. They have no vision, and when there is no vision the people perish...

"The money-changers have fled from their high seats in the temple of our civilization. We may now restore that temple to the ancient truths. The measure of the restoration lies in the extent to which we apply social values more noble than mere monetary profit...

"Happiness lies not in the mere possession of money; it lies in the joy of achievement, in the thrill of creative effort. The joy and moral stimulation of work, no longer must be forgotten in the mad chase of evanescent profits. These dark days will be worth all they cost us if they teach us that our true destiny is not to be ministered unto, but to minister to ourselves and to our fellow men.

"Our greatest primary task is to put people to work. This is no unsolvable problem if we face it wisely and courageously. It can be accomplished in part by direct recruiting by the Government itself, treating the task as we would treat the emergency of a war, but at the same time, through this employment, accomplishing greatly needed projects to stimulate and reorganize the use of our natural resources...

"There are many ways in which it can be helped, but it can never be helped merely by talking about it. We must act and act quickly...

"Finally, in our progress toward a resumption of work, we require two safeguards against a return of the evils of the old order; there must be a strict supervision of all banking and credits and investments; there must be an end to speculation with other people's money, and there must be provision for an adequate but sound currency...

"Action in this image and to this end is feasible under the form of government which we have inherited from our ancestors. Our Constitution is so simple and practical that it is possible always to meet extraordinary needs by changes in emphasis and arrangement without loss of essential form. That is why our constitutional system has proved itself the most superbly enduring political mechanism the modern world has produced. It has met every stress of vast expansion of territory, of foreign wars, of bitter internal strife, of world relations..."

First Fireside Chat (on Banking), March 12th, 1933

"By the afternoon of March 3d scarcely a bank in the country was open to do business. Proclamations temporarily closing them in whole or in part had been issued by the Governors in almost all the States...

"It was then that I issued the proclamation providing for the nationwide bank holiday, and this was the first step in the Government's reconstruction of our financial and economic fabric...

"The second step was the legislation promptly and patriotically passed by the Congress confirming my proclamation and broadening my powers so that it became possible in view of the requirement of time to extend the holiday and lift the ban of that holiday gradually. This law also gave authority to develop a program of rehabilitation of our banking facilities. I want to tell our citizens in every part of the Nation that the national Congress—Republicans and Democrats alike—showed by this action a devotion to public welfare and a realization of the emergency and the necessity for speed that it is difficult to match in our history...

"The third stage has been the series of regulations permitting the banks to continue their functions to take care of the distribution of food and household necessities and the payment of payrolls...

"We had a bad banking situation. Some of our bankers had shown themselves either incompetent or dishonest in their handling of the people's funds. They had used the money entrusted to them in speculations and unwise loans. This was, of course, not true in the vast majority of our banks, but it was true in enough of them to shock the people for a time into a sense of insecurity and to put them into a frame of mind where they did not differentiate, but seemed to assume that the acts of a comparative few had tainted them all. It was the Government's job to straighten out this situation and do it as quickly as possible. And the job is being performed...

"I do not promise you that every bank will be reopened or that individual losses will not be suffered, but there will be no losses that possibly could be avoided; and there would have been more and greater losses had we continued to drift. I can even promise you salvation for some at least of the sorely pressed banks. We shall be engaged not merely in reopening sound banks but in the creation of sound banks through reorganization..."

Annual Message to Congress, January 4th, 1935

"We find our population suffering from old inequalities, little changed by vast sporadic remedies. In spite of our efforts and in spite of our talk, we have not weeded out the over privileged and we have not effectively lifted up the underprivileged. Both of these manifestations of injustice have retarded happiness. No wise man has any intention of destroying what is known as the profit motive; because by the profit motive we mean the right by work to earn a decent livelihood for ourselves and for our families...

"We have, however, a clear mandate from the people, that Americans must forswear that conception of the acquisition of wealth which, through excessive profits, creates undue private power over private affairs and, to our misfortune, over public affairs as well. In building toward this end we do not destroy ambition, nor do we seek to divide our wealth into equal shares on stated occasions. We continue to recognize the greater ability of some to earn more than others. But we do assert that the ambition of the individual to obtain for him and his a proper security, a reasonable leisure, and a decent living throughout life, is an ambition to be preferred to the appetite for great wealth and great power...

"I recall to your attention my message to the Congress last June in which I said: "among our objectives I place the

security of the men, women and children of the Nation first."
That remains our first and continuing task; and in a very
real sense every major legislative enactment of this
Congress should be a component part of it...

"In defining immediate factors which enter into our
quest, I have spoken to the Congress and the people of three
great divisions:

1. The security of a livelihood through the better use of
the national resources of the land in which we live.

2. The security against the major hazards and vicissitudes
of life.

3. The security of decent homes.

"I am now ready to submit to the Congress a broad
program designed ultimately to establish all three of these
factors of security —a program which because of many lost
years will take many future years to fulfill."

Annual Message to Congress, January 3rd, 1936

"In March, 1933, I appealed to the Congress of the United
States and to the people of the United States in a new effort
to restore power to those to whom it rightfully belonged. The
response to that appeal resulted in the writing of a new
chapter in the history of popular government. You, the
members of the Legislative branch, and I, the Executive,
contended for and established a new relationship between
Government and people...

"What were the terms of that new relationship? They
were an appeal from the clamor of many private and selfish
interests, yes, an appeal from the clamor of partisan
interest, to the ideal of the public interest. Government
became the representative and the trustee of the public
interest. Our aim was to build upon essentially democratic

institutions, seeking all the while the adjustment of burdens, the help of the needy, the protection of the weak, the liberation of the exploited and the genuine protection of the people's property...

"It goes without saying that to create such an economic constitutional order, more than a single legislative enactment was called for. We, you in the Congress and I as the Executive, had to build upon a broad base. Now, after thirty-four months of work, we contemplate a fairly rounded whole. We have returned the control of the Federal Government to the City of Washington...

"To be sure, in so doing, we have invited battle. We have earned the hatred of entrenched greed. The very nature of the problem that we faced made it necessary to drive some people from power and strictly to regulate others. I made that plain when I took the oath of office in March, 1933. I spoke of the practices of the unscrupulous money-changers who stood indicted in the court of public opinion. I spoke of the rulers of the exchanges of mankind's goods, who failed through their own stubbornness and their own incompetence. I said that they had admitted their failure and had abdicated...

"Abdicated? Yes, in 1933, but now with the passing of danger they forget their damaging admissions and withdraw their abdication...

"They seek the restoration of their selfish power. They offer to lead us back round the same old corner into the same old dreary street...

"Yes, there are still determined groups that are intent upon that very thing. Rigorously held up to popular examination, their true character presents itself. They steal the livery of great national constitutional ideals to serve discredited special interests. As guardians and trustees for great groups of individual stockholders they wrongfully seek to carry the property and the interests entrusted to them into the arena of partisan politics. They seek-this minority in business and industry—to control and often do control and use for their own purposes legitimate and highly honored business associations; they engage in vast propaganda to spread fear and discord among the people— they would "gang up" against the people's liberties...

"The principle that they would instill into government if they succeed in seizing power is well shown by the principles which many of them have instilled into their own affairs: autocracy toward labor, toward stockholders, toward consumers, toward public sentiment. Autocrats in smaller things, they seek autocracy in bigger things. "By their fruits ye shall know them."

"Members of the Congress, let these challenges be met. If this is what these gentlemen want, let them say so to the Congress of the United States. Let them no longer hide their dissent in a cowardly cloak of generality. Let them define the issue. We have been specific in our affirmative action. Let them be specific in their negative attack...

"But the challenge faced by this Congress is more menacing than merely a return to the past—bad as that would be. Our resplendent economic autocracy does not want to return to that individualism of which they prate, even though the advantages under that system went to the ruthless and the strong. They realize that in thirty-four months we have built up new instruments of public power. In the hands of a people's Government this power is wholesome and proper. But in the hands of political puppets of an economic autocracy such power would provide shackles for the liberties of the people. Give them their way and they will take the course of every autocracy of the past —power for themselves, enslavement for the public."

Address to the Democratic National Convention in Philadelphia, June 27, 1936

"It was natural and perhaps human that the privileged princes of these new economic dynasties, thirsting for power, reached out for control over government itself. They created a new despotism and wrapped it in the robes of legal sanction. In its service new mercenaries sought to regiment the people, their labor, and their property. And as a result the average man once more confronts the problem that faced the Minute Man.

"Against economic tyranny such as this, the American citizen could appeal only to the organized power of government. The collapse of 1929 showed up the despotism for what it was. The election of 1932 was the people's mandate to end it. Under that mandate it is being ended.

"The royalists of the economic order have conceded that political freedom was the business of the government, but they have maintained that economic slavery was nobody's business. They granted that the government could protect the citizen in his right to vote, but they denied that the government could do anything to protect the citizen in his right to work and his right to live...

"These economic royalists complain that we seek to overthrow the institutions of America. What they really complain of is that we seek to take away their power. Our allegiance to American institutions requires the overthrow of this kind of power. In vain they seek to hide behind the flag and the Constitution. In their blindness they forget what the flag and the Constitution stand for. Now, as always, they stand for democracy, not tyranny; for freedom, not subjection; and against a dictatorship by mob rule and the over-privileged alike."

Annual Message to Congress, January 6th, 1937

"It is worth our while to read and reread the preamble of the Constitution, and Article I thereof which confers the legislative powers upon the Congress of the United States. It is also worth our while to read again the debates in the Constitutional Convention of one hundred and fifty years ago. From such reading, I obtain the very definite thought that the members of that Convention were fully aware that civilization would raise problems for the proposed new Federal Government, which they themselves could not even surmise; and that it was their definite intent and expectation that a liberal interpretation in the years to come would give to the Congress the same relative powers over new national problems as they themselves gave to the Congress over the national problems of their day...

"In presenting to the Convention the first basic draft of the Constitution, Edmund Randolph explained that it was the purpose 'to insert essential principles only, lest the operation of government should be clogged by rendering those provisions permanent and unalterable which ought to be accommodated to times and events'...

"With a better understanding of our purposes, and a more intelligent recognition of our needs as a Nation, it is not to be assumed that there will be prolonged failure to bring legislative and judicial action into closer harmony. Means must be found to adapt our legal forms and our judicial interpretation to the actual present national needs of the largest progressive democracy in the modern world."

State of the Union Message to Congress, January 11th, 1944

"This Republic had its beginning, and grew to its present strength, under the protection of certain inalienable political rights—among them the right of free speech, free press, free worship, trial by jury, freedom from unreasonable searches and seizures. They were our rights to life and liberty.

"As our Nation has grown in size and stature, however—as our industrial economy expanded—these political rights proved inadequate to assure us equality in the pursuit of happiness...

"We have come to a clear realization of the fact that true individual freedom cannot exist without economic security and independence. "Necessitous men are not free men." People who are hungry and out of a job are the stuff of which dictatorships are made...

"In our day these economic truths have become accepted as self-evident. We have accepted, so to speak, a second Bill of Rights under which a new basis of security and prosperity can be established for all regardless of station, race, or creed.

"Among these are:

• The right to a useful and remunerative job in the industries or shops or farms or mines of the Nation;

• The right to earn enough to provide adequate food and clothing and recreation;

• The right of every farmer to raise and sell his products at a return which will give him and his family a decent living;

• The right of every businessman, large and small, to trade in an atmosphere of freedom from unfair competition and domination by monopolies at home or abroad;

• The right of every family to a decent home;

• The right to adequate medical care and the opportunity to achieve and enjoy good health;

• The right to adequate protection from the economic fears of old age, sickness, accident, and unemployment;

• The right to a good education.

"All of these rights spell security. And after this war is won we must be prepared to move forward, in the implementation of these rights, to new goals of human happiness and well-being.

"America's own rightful place in the world depends in large part upon how fully these and similar rights have been carried into practice for our citizens. For unless there is security here at home there cannot be lasting peace in the world...

"One of the great American industrialists of our day—a man who has rendered yeoman service to his country in this crisis-recently emphasized the grave dangers of "rightist reaction" in this Nation. All clear-thinking businessmen share his concern. Indeed, if such reaction should develop— if history were to repeat itself and we were to return to the so-called "normalcy" of the 1920's—then it is certain that even though we shall have conquered our enemies on the battlefields abroad, we shall have yielded to the spirit of Fascism here at home...

"I ask the Congress to explore the means for implementing this economic bill of rights- for it is definitely the responsibility of the Congress so to do. Many of these problems are already before committees of the Congress in the form of proposed legislation. I shall from time to time communicate with the Congress with respect to these and further proposals. In the event that no adequate program of progress is evolved, I am certain that the Nation will be conscious of the fact."

Bibliography:

Selected writings of Lyndon LaRouche

"The End of Our Delusion," LaRouche PAC, 2007
"Music & Statecraft, How Space Is Organized," *Executive Intelligence Review*, Sept 14,2007
"Man & the Skies Above," *Executive Intelligence Review*, June 1, 2007
"Laputa's President Bush," *Executive Intelligence Review*, May 10, 2002
"How Bertrand Russell Became an Evil Man," *Fidelio*, Vol 3, No 3
"How to Think in a Time of Crisis," *Fidelio*, Vol. 7, No. 1
"The Truth About Temporal Eternity," *Fidelio*, Vol. 3, No. 2

General Bibliography

The Ghost Seer, by Friedrich Schiller, "Friedrich Schiller, Poet of Freedom," New Benjamin Franklin House, New York, 1985
The Bravo, by James Fenimore Cooper
Othello, by William Shakespeare
The "History" (Plantagenet) Plays, including Henry IV, Henry V, Henry VI, and Richard III, by William Shakespeare
Venice: Its Individual History from the Earliest Beginnings to the Fall of the Republic, by Pompeo Molmenti, Bergamo, Istituto Italiano D'Arti Grafiche, 1907
Original historical documents, available at the Avalon Project, can be found at http://www.yale.edu/lawweb/avalon/
Articles from the *New Federalist* can be found at: http://members.tripod.com/~american_almanac/contents.htm
Articles from the *Executive Intelligence Review* be found at: http://www.larouchepub.com
Articles from *Fidelio* can be found at: http://www.schillerinstitute.org/fid_97-01/fidelio.html

Bibliography - Individual Chapters

Preface

The Legislation of Lycurgus and Solon – by Friedrich Schiller, "Friedrich Schiller, Poet of Freedom, Vol. II," Schiller Institute, Washington, D.C. 1988

Prometheus Bound, by Aeschylus

The Three Principles of the People, by Sun-Yat Sen, 1924

The Harmony of Interests, by Henry C. Carey

The Declaration of Independence

The Constitution of the United States

"The true story behind the fall of the House of Windsor," *Executive Intelligence Review*, September, 1997

I. The Bestial View of Man: from Rome to Venice

Corpus Juris Civilis

The Domesday Book (The Norman Census)

Concordantia Catholica, by Nicholas of Cusa

II. The Venetian Empire, before and after the Council of Florence

The Medieval Supercompanies: A Study of the Peruzzi Company of Florence, by Edwin Hunt, Cambridge University Press, 1994

The Mediterranean and the Mediterranean World in the Age of Philip II, Vols. 1 & 2, by Fernand Braudel, University of California Press, Berkeley, 1995

De Monarchia, by Dante Alighieri

On Learned Ignorance, by Nicholas of Cusa

Toscanelli and Columbus. The letter and chart of Toscanelli on the route to the Indies by way of the west, sent in 1474 to the Portuguese Fernam Martins, and later on to Christopher Columbus, by Henry Vignaud, London, Sands & Co., 1902

"How The Venetians Took Over England and Created Freemasonry," by Gerry Rose, September, 1993, available at http://american_almanac.tripod.com/venfreem.htm

III. The Giovani Revolution

History of the Council of Trent, 1619, by Paolo Sarpi

History of the Inquisition, by Paolo Sarpi

Did Genoa and Venice Kick a Financial Revolution in the Quattrocento, by Michele Fratianni & Franco Spinelli, Oesterreichische Nationalbank

Advice Given to the Republic of Venice: how they ought to govern themselves both at home and abroad, to have perpetual Dominion, published in London in 1693, by Paolo Sarpi

Money and Banking in Medieval and Renaissance Venice, by Frederick C. Lane and Reinhold C. Mueller, Johns Hopkins University Press, Baltimore, 1985

IV. Sarpi's Web

Europae Speculum, 1598, by Sir Edwin Sandys

News Networks in 17th Century Britain and Europe, by JoanRaymond, Rutledge Press, 2006

Wotton And His Worlds: Spying, Science And Venetian Intrigues, by Gerald Curzon, Xlibris Corporation, 2004

Jacobean Gentleman: Sir Edwin Sandys, 1561-1629, by Theodore Rabb, Princeton, 1998

Aspects of Hobbes, by Noel Malcolm, Oxford University Press, 2002

V. Empiricism against the Renaissance

Pensieri, by Paolo Sarpi

The Dialogue Concerning Two Chief World Systems, 1630, and *The Discourses on Two New Sciences*, 1638, both by Galileo Galilei

Paolo Sarpi: Between Renaissance and Enlightenment, by David Wooten, Cambridge, 1983

Johannes Kepler's *New Astronomy*, http://wlym.com/~animations/newastronomy.html

Johannes Kepler's *The Harmony of the World*, http://wlym.com/~animations/harmonies/site.php?goto=intro.html

Hobbes, Locke, and Confusion's Masterpiece: An Examination of Seventeenth-Century Political Philosophy, by Ross Harrison, Cambridge University Press, 2003

Gassendi the Atomist: Advocate of History in an Age of Science, By Lynn Sumida Joy, Cambridge University Press, 2002

"Thomas Hobbes and His Disciples in France and England," by Quentin Skinner, *Comparative Studies in Society and History*, Vol. 8, No. 2, (1966)

Galileo, Hobbes, and the Book of Nature, by Douglas M. Jesseph, North Carolina State University

*"Thomas Hobbes and the Duke of Newcastle: A Study in the Mutuality of Patronage before the
Establishment of the Royal Society,"* by Lisa T. Sarasohn, *Isis*, Vol. 90, No. 4, (1999),

The Calvinist Copernicans: The Reception of the New Astronomy in the Dutch Republic, by Rienk Vermij, Amsterdam: Edita KNAW

"The Invention of the Telescope," by Albert Van Helden, *Transactions of the American Philosophical Society*, Vol. 67, No. 4

"Science and Patronage: Galileo and the Telescope", by Richard Westfall, *Isis*, vol. 76, no. 1, March, 1985

"Galileo's First Telescopes at Padua and Venice," by Stillman Drake, *Isis*, Vol. 50, No. 3

VI. The Theorists of the Oligarchical Model

Tractatus de Legibus, by Francisco Suarez

De Juri Belli Libri Ires, by Alberico Gentili

Politics, by Johannes Althusius

De Jure Praedae Commentaris; The Antiquity of the Ancient Batavians; De Jure Belli ac Pacis, all by Hugo Grotius

Two Treatises on Government, by John Locke

The School of Salamanca; Readings in Spanish Monetary Theory, 1544-1605, by Marjorie Grice-Hutchinson, Oxford University Press. 1952

Early Economic Thought in Spain, by Marjorie Grice-Hutchinson, G. Allen & Unwin, 1978

De Indis et de Ivre Belli Reflectiones, 1532, by Francisco de Vitoria

Comentarios de Usura, 1556, by Martin de Azpilcueta Navarro

De justitia et jure, 1605, by Leonard de Leys (Lessius)

Vindiciae contra tyrannos, 1579, by Phillipe du Plessis-Mornay

Memoirs of Algernon Sidney, by George Wilson Meadley, printed by Thomas Davison, 1813

Discourses Concerning Government, by Algernon Sidney

VII. The New Venice in Amsterdam

The History of the Revolt of the Netherlands, by Frederick Schiller

Political Balance; Political Discourses, both by Johan and Pieter de la Court

The Bank of Amsterdam and the Leap to Central Bank Money, by Stephen Quinn and William Roberds

John DeWitt, the Grand Pensionary of Holland, by M. Antonin Lefevre Pontalis, Longmans, Green & Co., London, 1885

"An Economic History of the Low Countries," by J.A. Van Houtte, *Journal of Modern History,* Vol 50, No 4, 1978

Completing a financial revolution: The finance of the Dutch East India trade and the rise of the Amsterdam capital market, 1595-1612, by Oscar Gelderblom and Joost Jonker, Utrecht University

VIII. Money, Speculation & Gambling

Confusion de Confusiones, by Joseph de la Vega (1688)

Money and Trade Considered, 1705, by John Law

Mare Liberum (The freedom of the seas), by Grotius

Some Considerations of the Consequences of the Lowering of Interest and Raising the Value of Money, by John Locke

Amsterdam as the cradle of modern futures and options trading, by Oscar Gelderblom and Joost Jonker, Utrecht University

A Financial Revolution in the Hapsburg Netherlands, by James Tracy, University of California Press, 1985

Roll the Bones: The History of Gambling, by David G. Schwartz, Gotham Books

"Scholastic Morality and the Birth of Economics: the Thought of Martin de Azpilcueta," by Rodrio Munoz de Juana, *Journal of Markets and Morality,* Vol. 4. No 1

"The Legal and Scholastic Roots of Leonardus Lessius Economic Thought," by Louis Baeck, *Journal of Economic Thought,* #37

From Commercial Arithmetic to Life Annuities: The Early History of Financial Economics, 1478-1776, by Geoffrey Poitras, Department of Economics and Statistics, National University of Singapore

IX. The Anglo-Dutch Empire

Declaration of Rights, 1689, by John Somers

The Life and Letters of Henry Wotton, by Logan Pearsall Smith, Oxford, Clarendon Press, 1907

A Discourse of Trade, 1690, by Nicholas Barbon

The Fable of the Bees, 1714, by Bernard Mandeville

Efficient Markets in the Eighteenth Century? Stock Exchanges in Amsterdam and London, by Larry Neal, University of Illinois at Urbana-Champaign

"Richard Cantillon, Financier to Amsterdam, July to November 1720," by Richard Hyse, *The Economic Journal,* Vol. 81, No. 324.

Anglo-Dutch Commerce and Finance in the 18th Century, by Charles Wilson, Cambridge, 1941

Mobilising resources for war: The Dutch and British financial revolutions compared, by Marjolein 't Hart, University of Amsterdam,

X. The Nature of the Beast

Dope, Inc. - Britain's Opium War Against the United States, by Kalimtgis, Goldman, and Steinberg, New Benjamin Franklin House, New York, 1978

The Chinese Opium Wars, by Jack Beeching, Harcourt, 1977

The Slave Trade, Domestic and Foreign: Why it Exists, and How it May Be Extinguished, by Henry C. Carey, 1853

The Vital Problem Facing China, by Sun Yat-Sen,

Queen Victoria's Little Wars, by Byron Farwell, W.W. Norton and Co., New York, 1985

Britain's Forgotten Wars: Colonial Campaigns of the 19th Century, by Ian Heron, Sutton Publishing, 2003

Late Victorian Holocausts, by Mike Davis, Verso Books, 2001

"How British Free Trade Starved Millions During Ireland's Potato Famine," by Paul Gallagher, *New Federalist*, May 29, 1995.

"The Role of Government Policy in Increasing Drug Use: Java, 1875-1914," by Siddharth Chandra, *The Journal of Economic History*, Vol. 62, No. 4 (Dec., 2002),

The Evolution of Central Banks, by Charles Goodhart, The MIT Press, 1988

Lombard Street, by Walter Bagehot

XI. The Commonwealth in America

The Mayflower Compact

A Model of Christian Charity, by John Winthrop, 1630

Bonifacius, An Essay upon the Good, by Cotton Mather, 1710

How the Nation Was Won: America's Untold Story; by H. Graham Lowry, Executive Intelligence Review, 1988

The Civil War and the American System, by W. Alan Salisbury, Campaigner Publications, 1978

"The Anti-Newtonian Roots of the American Revolution," by Phil Valenti, *Executive Intelligence Review*, Dec. 1, 1995. A version of this article is available at

http://members.tripod.com/~american_almanac/leiblock.htm#edit
or

"From Leibniz to Franklin on 'Happiness,'" by David Shavin, *Fidelio*, Vol. 12, No, 1, Summer 2003

"Life, Liberty, and The Pursuit of Happiness: How the Natural Law Concept of Gottfried Wilhelm Leibniz Inspired America's Founding Fathers," by Robert Trout, *Fidelio*, Vol. 6 No.1 , Spring, 1997

"A Temple of Hope, a Beacon of Liberty," by Robert Ingraham, *Executive Intelligence Review*, Oct. 27, 2006

New Essays on Human Understanding, by Gottfried Leibniz, 1704

Essay Concerning Human Understanding, by John Locke

Financial Crises: Their causes and effects, Henry C. Carey, 1864

Miscellaneous Works of Henry C. Carey, 1872

How to Outdo England Without Fighting Her, by Henry C. Carey, 1865

The National System of Political Economy, by Friedrich List

Outlines of American Political Economy, by Friedrich List, Dr. Bottiger Verlags-GmbH, Wiesbaden,

Nothing Like It In The World: The Men who Built the Transcontinental Railroad, 1863-1869. by Stephen E. Ambrose, Simon and Schuster, 2000

The Three Principles of the People, by Sun-Yat Sen

As He Saw It, by Elliott Roosevelt, Duell, Sloan and Pearce, 1946

"1932," video, available at http://www.larouchepac.com

An Introduction to the Principles of Morals and Legislation, by Jeremy Bentham, 1781, published by Batoche Books, Kitchener, 2000

XII. Richard Nixon's Treason: the post-1971 world

"Fascism and the Project For a World Company," by John Hoefle, *Executive Intelligence Review*, February 29, 2008

"Dead Crocodiles Found Beached On the Queen's Cayman Islands," by John Hoefle, *Executive Intelligence Review*, September 21, 2007

Confessions of an Economic Hitman, by John Perkins, Berrett-Koehler Publishers, 2004

"Yes! It Really is Gambling," by Robert Ingraham, *Executive Intelligence Review*, July 27, 2007, available at

http://www.larouchepub.com/other/2007/3429it_is_gambling.ht
ml

The Homeowner and Bank Protection Act of 2007, available at
http://www.larouchepac.com

Doom has Struck! Three Steps to Survival, by Lyndon LaRouche,
at LaRouche PAC.

Index

A

Adam Smith, 80, 119, 217, 218, 219, 236, 239, 248, 261, 262

Algernon Sidney, 134, 135, 284

Althusius, Johannes, 118, 125, 126, 127, 133, 284

Amsterdam Bourse, 60. 147, 148, 162, 164, 168, 178

Antonio Conti, 107, 185

Aristotle, 28, 33, 34, 43, 46, 84, 86, 87, 117, 197

asentio, 188

Ashley Cooper, Anthony, 134, 136, 176

B

Bagehot, Walter, 187, 286

Baldassare Capra, 96

Bank of Amsterdam, 58, 60, 145, 147, 162, 163, 179, 189, 284

Bank of International Settlements, 217

Bank of Venice, 53, 57, 58, 145, 147, 180

Beeckman, Isaac, 93, 99, 100, 101, 102

Benjamin Franklin, 16, 22, 205, 223, 225, 229, 281, 286

Bentham, Jeremy, 80, 218, 226, 239, 262, 287

Bernanke, Ben, 251

Bertrand Russell, 15, 16, 80, 196, 263, 281

Beza, Theodore, 74, 120

Bilderberg Society, 252

Black Guelph party, 40, 47

Boccaccio, Giovanni, 43

Bolingbroke, Henry St. John, 184, 185

Botero, Giovanni, 137

Bretton Woods agreement, 20, 246, 248, 257

British East India Company, 146, 190

Buchanan, George, 120

C

Calvin, Jean, 71, 74, 75, 120

Cantillon, Richard, 190, 285

Cardano, Girolamo , 168

Carey, Henry, 17, 197, 198, 202, 203, 214, 234, 237, 241, 282, 286, 287

Casa di San Giorgio, 57

Casaubon, Isaac, 69, 75, 151

Cavendish family, 62, 68, 69, 74, 75, 76, 103, 104, 105, 106, 136, 170, 175

Cecil family, 69, 178

Charlemagne, 33, 35, 39

Charles II, 135

Churchill, Winston, 175, 231, 234, 245

Colet, John, 178

Columbus, Christopher, 44, 46, 111, 198, 282

Confusion de Confusiones, 159, 165, 285

Contarini, Gasparo, 48, 55, 56, 95

Covarrubias, Diego de, 117

Cremonini, Cesare, 87

Cusa, Nicholas of, 26, 31, 32, 43, 44, 45, 46, 48, 54, 67, 80, 81, 86, 89, 120, 137, 282

D

da Vinci, Leonardo, 92

Dante Alighieri, 42, 80, 282

David Hilbert, 263

de Dominis, Marco Antonio, 70, 72, 73, 85, 96

de la Court brothers, 152, 153, 284

de la Vega, Joseph, 159, 165, 285

de Menchaca, Fernando Vasquez, 115, 133

de Moivre, Abraham, 168, 170

de Soto, Domingo, 115, 137

de Vattel, Emmerich, 225, 228

de Vitoria, Francisco, 110, 111, 112, 113, 137, 284

Descartes, Rene, 81, 84, 99, 100, 101, 102, 103, 105, 106, 152, 153, 168, 226

DeWitt brothers, 102, 103, 134, 136, 137, 151, 152, 154, 169, 285

Diocletian, 27, 197

Diodoti, Giovanni, 66, 74

Donato, Leonardo, 55, 56, 69

Dope, Inc., 205, 286

Du Bois, W.E.B., 200

Dutch East India Company, 145
Dutch West India Company, 143, 190, 198

E

East India Company, 60, 67, 123, 124, 126, 145, 148, 150, 162, 177, 178, 179, 180, 182, 183, 184, 188, 189, 190, 199, 206, 207, 238, 248
Edmund Halley, 137, 169, 171
Elizabeth I, 178
Elmina fortress, 198
Erasmus, 46, 49, 142, 178
Erich Raspe, 225
European Central Bank, 217

F

Fenimore Cooper, James, 3, 281
Fermat, Pierre, 100
Francis Bacon, 56, 62, 69, 72, 101, 104, 137, 170, 186
Frederick V, 61
Fugger, House of, 47, 142, 144

G

Galileo Galilei, 56, 69, 76, 80, 81, 83, 85, 87, 88, 89, 90, 91, 92, 93, 94, 95, 96, 97, 98, 99, 100, 101, 102, 103, 104, 105, 107, 137, 168, 283, 284
Gassendi, Pierre, 98, 100, 101, 105, 106, 283
GATT, 247
Gentili, Alberico, 69, 72, 118, 123, 125, 126, 127, 186, 284
George Ball, 252
George Bush, 201
Giotto Bondone, 43
Giovani Party, 4, 18, 55, 57, 58, 60, 69, 97, 113, 179
Glass-Steagall Act, 159, 240, 250
gold standard, 211, 213, 215
Gotthold Lessing, 225
Gouverneur Morris, 80
Greenspan, Alan, 251
Grotius, Hugo, 32, 33, 73, 74, 75, 100, 102, 112, 118, 123, 124, 125, 126, 134, 150, 151, 197, 226, 284, 285

H

H.G Wells, 80
Hamilton, Alexander, 4, 10, 20, 22, 147, 159, 221, 231, 232, 234, 236, 237, 238, 239, 241, 247, 257, 262, 264, 266, 293
Hayek, Friedrich, 4, 12, 112, 260, 261, 262, 263, 266
Henry Sidney, 136, 155, 175
Hitler, Adolf, 195, 203
Hobbes, Thomas, 68, 69, 74, 75, 76, 99, 100, 101, 103, 104, 105, 106, 153, 170, 226, 264, 283, 284
Hoefle, John, 253, 287
Hotman, Francois, 71, 84, 120, 123, 127
Huxley family, 80
Huygens, Christian, 100

J

James I, 61, 62, 66, 75, 179
James II, 155
James Mill, 262
John F. Kennedy, 196, 245
John Law, 117, 119, 167, 249, 285
John Robinson, 16, 227
John Stuart Mill, 80, 239, 262
Jonathan Swift, 183, 184
Josiah Child, 183
Justinian, Emperor, 25, 27, 30, 32, 39

K

Kästner, Abraham, 225
Kepler, Jonannes, 81, 83, 88, 89, 90, 95, 97, 99, 100, 102, 107, 169, 283
Keynes, John Maynard, 4, 260, 261, 262, 263, 266

L

Languet, Hubert, 120, 143
LaRouche, Lyndon, 16, 54, 81, 82, 88, 111, 217, 225, 246, 247, 256, 257, 265, 281, 288, 293
Leibniz, Gottfried, 96, 107, 169, 171, 225, 226, 228, 264, 287
Lessius, Leonard de Lays, 116, 118, 137, 284, 285

127, 143, 151, 153, 168, 169, 170,
171, 179, 200, 224, 226, 282, 283
Schiller, Friedrich, 49, 59, 142, 281, 282,
284
Shakespeare, William, 174, 178, 179,
281
Simon Marius, 93, 96, 97
Somers, John, 135, 285
St. Augustine, 29
Suarez, Francisco, 118, 123, 127, 284
Sun-Yat Sen, 20, 282, 287

T

Thatcher, Margaret, 201
Thomas More, 46, 49, 178
Toffler, Alvin, 19
Torquemada, Tomas de, 48
Toscanelli, 44, 282
Tostado, Alfonso, 113
Treaty of Utrecht, 189, 199
Truman, Harry, 245
Tulipmania, 165

V

Van Buren, Martin, 237, 239
Van Eyck, Jan, 142
Virginia Company, 66, 68, 76, 104, 183,
200

VOC, 123, 124, 145, 146, 147, 148, 164,
181, 184, 189, 198, 199
von Dohna, Christoph von, 61
von Mises, Ludwing, 112, 261, 264
von Münchausen, Baron, 225

W

Walpole, Horace, 185
Walsingham, Thomas, 69, 178
Washington, George, 223, 261, 262,
274, 282
William of Orange, 105, 128, 135, 136,
171, 175, 180
William Paterson, 180
William Petty, 105, 137, 169, 170, 179,
187, 265
William Russell, 135, 136
William Temple, 134
William the Silent, 59, 143, 144
Winthrop, John, 16, 136, 223, 227, 286
Wisselbank, 141, 145, 147, 163, 181,
190
Wotton, Henry, 61, 62, 68, 69, 72, 74,
75, 90, 103, 104, 179, 283, 285

Z

Zabarella, Giacomo, 87

ABOUT THE AUTHOR

Robert Ingraham is a political organizer, author and historian, specializing in studies of the British Empire, the American Revolution, Abraham Lincoln, Alexander Hamilton and the Florentine Renaissance. He was a friend of Lyndon LaRouche for five decades. Originally from New York City, he comes from a blue-collar background, and he currently resides in Oakland, California with his wife Andrea.